GREEK MYTHOLOGY

Gods, Heroes, Monsters and Stories

Richard Michael Schlesinger

To Hurmar, and all the other minotaurs

INTRODUCTION

Shoes, shrinks and spacecrafts

Although its origins date back to more than 2500 years ago, greek mythology is still all around us. It has never really left the western civilization, in fact, we can consider it one of its, more or less visible, pillars. Just by a quick look around, we can see the signs of this ancient mythology in our present everyday life. Some are deeply rooted in our higher culture, others have just become a sort of pop icon, and in some cases, they are so part of our lives that we don't even know, or notice anymore, about their ancient greek origins.

Just think about modern psychology, which, starting with its own name which derives from the character of Psyche, is full of references to Greek mythology, like the Oedipus complex, just to mention the most famous.

Planets are named after Roman divinities, but we know they are the same Greek gods with different names, Jupiter, Venus, Mercury, are none other than Zeus, Aphrodite, and Hermes. And also most stars and constellations, like Ursa major and Ursa minor, or Orion and Scorpio, got their names from ancient Greek origin stories. And while we are in space, a lot of space missions or spacecraft are named after Greek mythology, like Apollo, Artemis (that was Apollo's twin sister), or Ulysses.

Pop culture too has always been full of Greek mythology references. Nowadays the first that comes to mind is probably the Percy Jackson saga, worldwide success with both books and movies, that narrates the adventures of the Olympus gods living in the contemporary world. But we can also think of Hercules, the Roman name of Heracles, brought by Disney to the silver screen in 1997, or Wonder Woman, whose origins were rewritten a few times like often happens to superheroes, but always involve Greek mythology, with the heroin either created from clay by the amazon Queen Hippolyta or born from Queen Hippolyta and Zeus. And Harry Potter's Centaurs too come straight from Greek myth.

Speaking of movies, you may be familiar with the winged horse in the logo of Tristar Pictures. We are talking about Pegasus, whose peculiar birth we will see in this book, and who, other than by Tristar Pictures has been frequently used on logos and graphics for airlines, stamps, gas stations, and a lot more. And of course, there are plenty of brands that have some greek mythology references in their names or iconographies. To name one, the most famous sneakers brand in the world is named after Nike, the Greek goddess of victory.

Pegasus the winged horse in Tristar Pictures and Mobil Oil Logos

And of course, being something that goes back thousands of years, greek mythology has also formed our language. Let's think of a way of saying like "opening Pandora's box", meaning creating a situation that leads to an unstoppable series of untold troubles, or even simple words like "echo", which derives from the mountain nymph Echo who fell in love with Narcissus, or Atlas, from the name of the titan who was condemned to carry the earth and the sky upon his shoulder, or even Hypnosis from Hypnos, the god of sleep. And even when we need to create new words we can turn to ancient Greek mythology, like in the case of computer malware disguised as legitimate software, that couldn't have a more exact name than "trojan horses".

A Good Story Can Be Just a Good Story

Now, these above are just a few examples, and quite shallow too, of how greek mythology is still present in our lives, often without us even noticing. The role of Greek myth in western civilization is, of course, way deeper than this, and there are many excellent books and essays about that. And they are super interesting, but this one is not one of those.

As the subtitle goes this is all about "gods, heroes, monsters and stories". Let's be clear: there is nothing wrong with going deep and behind the hidden meanings and philosophical questions related to Greek mythology. In fact, it was studying these topics, and loving it, that I noticed that it wasn't easy to find books with just the stories. Like if they were too famous to be told again. So most of the books just quickly mention the story and dive deep into the interpretations.

And again, nothing wrong with it, I was just missing something: the pure, innocent, childish pleasure of the stories. Just the stories, pure and simple, and in today's language. Because let's say it, these are damn good stories.

And what do you do when you would like to read a book that you can find? Well, you write it! So here it is, I hope you'll enjoy reading this as much as I enjoyed writing it.

RMS

THE TWELVE OLYMPIANS

Welcome to Mount Olympus. The Pantheon of the Greek deities. Here, according to Greek mythology, used to live the deities who ruled on all the aspects of the Universe. The deities of Olympus were also known as the twelve Olympians, or under the greek name of Dodekatheon, the twelve gods.

Depending on different periods and traditions, we have more than twelve deities that have been members of the

Twelve Olympians Club. This does not mean that in some periods we have the thirteen or the fourteen Olympians. The Dodekatheon stayed, but someone would put in some gods, someone some others. I won't make a choice of my favorites and will introduce you to the main ones. Here to you, the Fourteen Twelve Olympians!

Zeus

 The god of the sky and the thunder. The chief of the Olympus. The god of gods, the father of all the gods and humans. The big boss up here on the Olympus. Usually represented with his symbols, the eagle and the thunderbolt. Other than ruling on Olympus and the earth his favorite pastime is to chase women - humans, goddesses, or nymphs - and hence get chased by his wife.

Hera

Zeus' wife, the queen of the Olympians, the goddess of marriage, women, childbirth, and family. As goddess of marriage and family, she was quite old school, so she was very jealous and vindictive, especially towards the lovers of her husband and their illegitimate offspring.

Poseidon

Brother of Zeus and Hades and father of Orion and Triton was the god of sea and water, but also of earthquakes and storms. He created horses. Poseidon was usually depicted on a chariot drawn by four fish-tailed horses, holding a trident.

Hades

The first-born son of Cronus and Rhea, older brother of Zeus and Poseidon, was the god of Tartarus, the underworld of Greek mythology, the realm of the dead. We can often see him accompanied by Cerberus, the three-headed dog that guarded the entrance of the Underworld.

Demeter

The goddess of agriculture, harvest, fertility, and sacred law. Sister of Zeus, she was frequently depicted with images of the harvest like flowers, grain or fruits, or with her daughter Persephone.

Athena

Daughter of Zeus, born from his forehead, was the goddess of wisdom, handicraft, and warfare. While being the goddess of wisdom she was a little touchy, and she may push it a little too far, sometimes. She is usually shown wearing a helmet and holding a spear, and sometimes a shield. She was the founder of Athens, as the name suggests.

Apollo

The god of a lot of things: music, poetry, art, oracles, truth, archery, plague, medicine, sun, light, and knowledge among others. He is the son of Zeus and Leto and the twin brother of Artemis. He is considered the most beautiful of all the gods.

Artemis

The twin sister of Apollo, goddess of the hunt, forests, hills, the moon, and archers, was patron and protector of the young girls. She is usually depicted with a bow and arrows, accompanied by a young deer.

Ares

The god of war. While his Roman version was very popular and worshipped, Ares was not. He was seen as the personification of the brutality of war and not of its alleged romantic side. Generally portrayed with a helmet, spear, and shield.

Aphrodite

The goddess of sexual love, beauty, and fertility, was married to Hephaestus but she was frequently unfaithful to him and had many lovers. She is often depicted nude or semi-nude.

Hephaestus

Aphrodites' husband and the god of fire, metalworking, stone masonry, forges, the art of sculpture, and blacksmiths. He was the son of Zeus and Hera, he is usually portrayed with his working tool, smith's hammer, anvil, and a pair of tongs.

Hermes

The gods' messenger, and the god of trade, thieves, luck, fertility, language, and travelers. He is one of the most iconic and recognizable gods, with his winged helmet and the caduceus, the winged staff entwined by two serpents that is still today the symbol of logistics.

Hestia

The virgin goddess of the hearth, the right ordering of domesticity, the family, the home, and the state. She received the first offering at every sacrifice in the household

Dionysus

The god of harvest, the vine, winemaking, wine, ritual madness, religious ecstasy, and theater. He was indifferently depicted as an older, long-bearded god, or as a young, long-haired, effeminate one. In both versions, though, he almost always has a drinking cup, a bunch of grapes, and a crown of ivy.

As we know ancient Greek and Roman mythologies are virtually the same. Basically, the only relevant difference is the different names of the characters. In this book, as you can easily imagine, you will always find the Greek version of the names (except for a few painting image captions that could keep the original roman name). Anyway, a quick recap table can be useful, so here it is.

GREEK NAME	ROMAN NAME
Zeus	Jupiter
Hera	Juno
Poseidon	Neptune
Hades	Pluto
Demeter	Ceres
Athena	Minerva
Apollo	Apollo
Artemis	Diana
Ares	Mars
Aphrodite	Venus
Hephaestus	Vulcan
Hermes	Mercury
Hestia	Vesta
Dionysus	Bacchus

Renée Antoine Houasse - *Birth of Minerva (Athena)* - 1686

The stories about the origins of the gods are both intriguing and horrifying. They tell us in great detail how Cronus castrated his father Uranus, but remain vague about how Chaos birthed the first batch of primordial deities from the original void of nothingness. So we won't get the answer to the first origin of the universe, but we still can learn about other beginnings, like how humans received the gift of fire, how Athena was born out of a head and Dionysus out of a thigh, and about how the world was a happy and easy place to live in before all of its problems came out all at once from a box. Or, to be more precise, a jar.

Cronus The Cannibal

The son of Uranus and Gaia, the Titan Cronus, learned from an oracle that one of his children would eventually unseat him as ruler of the Titans. This shouldn't have been surprising news to him since he had done precisely the same thing with his father, Uranus.

Anyway, he didn't want the same thing to happen to him, so when Rhea gave birth to their children, the Titan did what every father worried about his sons eventually stealing its throne would have done: he ate them.

Giovanni Francesco Romanelli - *Chronos* - second quarter of 17th century

One by one, he devoured Rhea's babies. No sooner had she given birth than he would grab the children and swallow them whole. Of course, the children stayed alive, they were immortal after all, but Rhea began to grow resentment towards Cronus. Women, right?

When the time came to deliver Zeus, she came up with a plan. She gave birth to him on Crete's island, without telling Cronus, and then hid him in a cave on Mount Ida. In his place, she wrapped a large stone in swaddling clothes and handed her fake newborn son to Cronus.

As expected, Cronus ate the rock, thinking it was Zeus. The real Zeus grew up in secret on Crete, raised by a divine goat, a nymph, or his grandmother Gaia (depending on the source). And when Zeus had grown into a powerful young deity, the cunning Titaness Metis gave him a magic potion. Zeus surprised Cronus and forced his father to drink the potion. Cronus became sick after drinking the potion and vomited.

Cronus threw up Zeus's siblings in reverse order. Hera, Poseidon, Demeter, Hades, and Hestia were all reborn. Eventually, they declared war on Cronus and the Titans, joining with the Hecatonchires and the Cyclopes to overthrow the Titans and take over as the new generation of gods and goddesses.

The Birth Of Athena

An oracle prophesied that one of the children of Metis, the Titaness of wisdom, would eventually supplant Zeus—just as Zeus had once overthrown Cronus, and just as Cronus had overthrown Uranus. The king of the gods took this warning seriously. He'd recently had a sexual relationship with Metis, and the moment he learned she was pregnant, Zeus took direct action. He swallowed the Titaness.

This gave him a terrible headache. The king of the gods wailed and moaned with the pain, and Hermes told Hephaestus (in different versions instead of Hephaestus, we can find Prometheus, Hermes, or Ares) to use one of his most powerful axes to split Zeus's head open (this only works for gods, don't try it at home). Out of the god's skull sprang Athena, fully formed, bearing a war shield and wearing a suit of armor. She unleashed a full-throated battle cry that made the gods tremble, but, contrary to the prediction of the oracle, she didn't overthrow him. Instead, Athena became the beloved goddess of wisdom and war, and one of Zeus's favorite children.

The Birth Of Hephaestus

All of Olympus' gods and goddesses were perfect and beautiful, so when Hera gave birth to an ugly child, the weak, sickly Hephaestus, Zeus was not happy about it. And neither was Hera. One of them (some versions say Zeus, some say Era, whatever, it's the gesture that counts) hurled the hideous baby off Mount Olympus in disgust.

Hephaestus tumbled through the air, falling for at least a day until he finally landed on the island of Lemnos. The fall left him crippled and bruised, but the sea goddess

Thetis found the little baby on her shores and cared for him. A tribe of craftsmen living on the island, the Sintians, taught Hephaestus to make beautiful things. He would always limp as a consequence of the fall, but he made a golden brace to help support his injured foot.

As Hephaestus grew strong and talented with the forge, blessed by amazing creativity, Zeus realized the mistake he made and finally invited the limping god back to Olympus. They equipped Hephaestus with a magic workshop where he created all the gods' and goddesses' best equipment, from Hermes's winged sandals to Aphrodite's magic girdle.

The Birth Of Dionysus

For a time, Zeus carried on a secret affair with Semele, a mortal princess of Thebes. But one night, Hera followed Zeus to earth and discovered their illicit union. The queen of the gods disguised herself as an older woman and spoke to Semele, who told her Zeus had gotten her pregnant.

"How do you know it's Zeus?" Hera asked. "Ask for proof. Demand to see him in all his divine splendor."

Suddenly, Semele felt doubtful about her lover. One day, she asked him to promise he would do anything for her. Under the effect of his infatuation, he swore by the river Styx. An unbreakable oath. Semele asked to see his true godly appearance, and, bound by the oath, Zeus had to obey. He cast off his human disguise and revealed himself in a powerful explosion of thunder and lightning. The fiery display incinerated Semele, as he'd known it would, but Zeus was able to rescue her unborn baby. He sewed the baby into his thigh and carried the gestation to term.

Caravaggio - *Bacchus* - 1596

Zeus went to an island where he released Dionysus, whose name means "twice-born," from his thigh. The child was raised by nymphs and Zeus made him one of the gods on Mount Olympus, the god of wine and celebrations.

According to other traditions, Dionysus was the son of Zeus and Persephone (or Demeter). In these versions, Hera recruited the Titans to kill the infant baby Dionysus by capturing his attention with toys and then tearing him to pieces. By the time Zeus arrived and drove off the Titans, the only part of Dionysus remaining was his heart. In this version of the two births of Dionysus, Zeus sewed the heart into his own thigh, and Dionysus grew again this way.

Pandora's Box

Epimetheus was a Titan, but he and his brother Prometheus had joined the gods of Olympus in their great battle against the Titans. As a way of expressing gratitude, Zeus asks Hephaestus to give Epimetheus a special gift: a mortal woman to become his wife. The artisan god fashioned Pandora out of the soil and the Four Winds breathed life into her body.

All the gods donated her their best blessings and gifts. Aphrodite gave her beauty, grace, and desire. Hermes, the messenger god, gave her a cunning, and bold mind. Athena clothed her and taught her to be deft with her hands. Poseidon bestowed on her a pearl necklace that would prevent her from drowning. Apollo taught her to play the lyre and to sing. Hera gave her the wiliest gift, curiosity. The name Pandora means "all-gifted."

Hermes delivered her to Epimetheus on earth, and the Titan was pleased. Modeled after Aphrodite's great beauty, Pandora looked like a goddess.

As he left the new bride with the grateful Titan, Hermes gave Pandora one last wedding gift. It was a small, jeweled box (actually a jar) with a special recommendation from Zeus never to open it.

Pandora and Epimetheus started their life together, but she couldn't keep her mind off that box. What could be inside it? The question could not get out of her mind. She fought against it, day after day until finally, she could fight the impulse no more. She opened the box.

John William Waterhouse - *Pandora* - 1896

As a parallel to the blessings they had given her, the gods had filled the box with all the worst things in life, to preserve her from them. Sorrow. Death. Lies. All these calamities rose into the air like birds, swirling into the world around her. Sickness arrived, as did insanity, famine, crime, greed, jealousy, and any other kind of evils. Realizing what she had done, Pandora immediately slammed the box shut. But it was too late. These terrible forces had been introduced to humanity and could never again be contained within the box. Suddenly the gift Hera gave her was not that great of a gift anymore.

Yet in the moment of shutting the terrible box, she trapped one last gift inside, that was exactly what humans needed to bear these burdens: hope.

The Four Winds breathed life into Pandora's body. Who were they? The Greeks assigned wind gods to each of the four cardinal directions. Together these minor deities were known as the Anemoi, and all four were the children of Eos, the goddess of dawn, and Aeolus, the keeper of the winds.

Boreas was the north wind, associated with winter. He was an old, bearded man who brought cold temperatures, and therefore wasn't very popular. His sons, the Boreads, were two of Jason's Argonauts.

Notus blew from the south and was associated with autumn. He brought the hot storms of late summer and fall, which generally were bad for crops. He wasn't very popular either.

 **Eurus**, the east wind, was not associated with any particular season. His wind often brought rain but was considered unlucky.

 **Zephyrus** was the gentle breeze from the west, associated with spring. He brought new life and blooming flowers, which made him highly regarded among the Greeks. Zephyrus was the husband of Iris, goddess of the rainbow.

In addition to these main four, other minor deities represented the winds coming from the northeast, northwest, southeast, and southwest.

THE SAGA OF PERSEUS

Giuseppe Cesari - *Perseus and Andromeda* - 1592

Danae and Perseus

Perseus was the son of Danae, the princess of Argos. Her father Acrisius, the king of Argos, was worried about his lack of male heirs, so he consulted the Oracle of Delphi. The Oracle foretold that one day he would be killed by his grandson and that Danae, his daughter would give birth to this grandson. Terrified that this prediction would come true, King Acrisius decided to keep Danae locked up in a chamber underground. This way, the king thought, she would never be able to meet a man and get pregnant, and the prophecy would not fulfill.

Now, you can hide your daughter as much as you want, but if it is from Zeus that you are hiding her, well, that's not an easy job. Because it happened that, locked away and sad, Danae caught the eye of Zeus. The great god of the Skies took pity on the poor princess and went to visit her, in the form of golden rain. Thus, he could easily get inside the tower where the princess was held. Once inside the chamber, Zeus managed to enter Danae's body and impregnate her, and out of this peculiar coupling Perseus was born.

When king Acrisius heard about Perseus, he remembered the prophecy and feared that it would come true. Since Zeus fathered the child, there was no way that he could kill him. Doing so would put him at the mercy of the furies, and as we learned thus far, the wrath of the gods is not something you want to trigger.

Then the King decided to send his daughter and grandson away instead of killing him, but he could not risk the child growing up and fulfilling the prophecy. So, to be sure that neither Perseus or Danae would never come near him again, he put both Danae and Perseus in a wooden box and cast them out to sea. He was sure that the pair would die in the rough waters. How this would be different, in the King's mind, from just killing the baby, is one of the many unanswered questions of Greek mythology.

But Zeus saw what was happening. He called out to his brother Poseidon and asked him to calm the sea. So, instead of perishing, Danae and her son Perseus made it to the shores of Seriphos safely. A man named Dictys, the brother of the Seriphos king, Polydectes, found the chest on the beach. He opened it and freed Danae and Perseus. Dictys took mother and son into his home, and he raised the boy as his own. Time passed, and Perseus grew into a fine figure of a man.

Giorgio Ghisi - *Danae and the Infant Perseus Cast out to Sea By Acrisius* - 1543

After some time, the king saw Perseus' mother, fell for her, and wanted to marry her. but Danae did not want to become Polydectes' bride. Perseus, which meanwhile had grown a strong young man, was an obstacle to the king's plan, defending Danae from his unwanted attention. So, to get rid of her son, the king, unable to beat him with the force, tried to use cunning.

So Polydectes came up with a way to shame Perseus and get him out of the way to have Danae for himself. First, Polydectes decided to throw a party to collect wedding gifts for his friend's daughter. Every guest was supposed to bring a donation of horses, but Perseus had no horses to give. Polydectes knew this, and he also knew that Perseus was honorable, brave, and healthy and that these things could be used against him.

Polydectes' plan was to humiliate Perseus, who came to the banquet without a gift. The young hero didn't want to dishonor either his host or the bridal couple so he made a promise to the King. He pledged that he would bring whatever gift the king wanted.

Polydectes felt that the moment had come. This was how he would get rid of Perseus once and for all. He told Perseus to bring him something that he was sure would be impossible for the young man to get. What exactly? We will see it soon...

Medusa the Gorgon

Medusa is undoubtedly one of the most well-known Greek Mythology antagonists. She and her two sisters, Stheno and Euryale, were known as the Gorgons. They were the sea god's children, Phorcys (Phorkys), and his sister, Ceto (Keto). The Gorgons had other siblings from Phorcys that, like them, were monsters that were to be reckoned with. One of these siblings was the three sea hags called the Graeae, who shared one eye.

Medusa, though, was a foe worthy of the bravest Greek heroes. While her appearance had been described as hideous, she had not always been so terrifying. Unlike her two sisters, Medusa was mortal, and she was once an extremely beautiful woman. She had piercing eyes that men could not help but sing praises about. Her long lustrous hair rivaled that of the goddesses, and many a suitor longed to run their fingers through her locks.

Gianlorenzo Bernini - *Medusa* - 1640

But Medusa would have none of it. Despite her numerous suitors, she instead became a priestess at one of the goddesses Athena's temples. Much to the frustration of the men who loved her, Medusa was unattainable. Priestesses at Athena's temple took a vow of celibacy, and they were to remain virgins for their entire lives.

While most of Medusa's admirers had given up on the virtuous priestess, there was one who would not take no for an answer. Poseidon, the sea god, still pursued the beautiful Medusa.

She ran to the temple to seek out the protection of Athena. She had thought that Poseidon would not touch her if she were within the walls of the temple. But she was wrong. Blinded by his passion, Poseidon ravished Medusa in Athena's temple.

There are some versions of the story where Medusa is not taken by force. She falls in love with the sea god as well, and instead of staying faithful to her vow of being celibate, she marries Poseidon. This is not the most common version of the story but is the one that makes Athena's reaction look a little less crazy.

Right, because when the goddess found out what happened, she became furious. In her eyes, Medusa had defiled her temple. As punishment, she turned her unfaithful priestess into a hideous being. The eyes that had once been admired by men became a curse to behold. Anyone who would make contact with Medusa's stare would immediately be turned to stone. The beautiful strands of her hair were transformed into horrific and venomous snakes.

Some stories say that despite the snakes and the gaze of stone, Medusa remained beautiful. Only this time, to look at her was deadly.

Medusa lived, in most of the versions, with her sisters in the Western Ocean close to the Hesperides. There are tales, though, that say the sisters lived in what is now known as Libya.

Polydectes' request

After she was turned into a monster, Medusa stayed with her sisters. Stories about them spread far and wide, so heroes came from all corners of the world to slay them. But despite their skills with weapons, Medusa turned them all to stone. Medusa, it seemed, could not be defeated.

King Polydectes saw a chance there, so he asked Perseus to bring back the head of Medusa. Since it was a quest that no hero had ever been able to do, he was sure that it was the perfect way to get rid of the young man. With Perseus dead, Polydectes would be free to marry Danae.

But Perseus was no ordinary hero: he was the son of Zeus. And he held the favor of the gods. Athena guided him on the quest by telling him to find the Hesperides. They were nymphs who lived at the very western edge of the world, tending a fantastic garden that held a tree that bore golden apples, which had been a wedding present from Hera to Zeus. Athena told Perseus the Hesperides would be able to help him defeat Medusa.

But to find the way to that divine garden, Perseus needed to find the Graeae, the Grey Ones. The Graeae were sisters of the Gorgons, three hideous older women who had but one eye they shared by passing it from one to the other. Perseus came to the cave of the Graeae. He watched the women passing the eye back and forth, taking turns using it to see.

Perseus hid in a dark corner, and when the eye was being passed from one old hag then, he jumped out and snatched it away. The Graeae wailed and screamed at Perseus, but he held firm: they would get their eye back if they took him to the garden of the Hesperides. Finally, the women realized they had to do as Perseus asked, so they took him to the park, and when they arrived there, Perseus gave them back their eye, as promised.

Henry Fuseli - *Perseus Returning the Eye to the Graiai* -

With the information he got from the Graeae, Perseus was
able to find the Hesperides. There he got a magic bag in
which he could put the head of Medusa. He also got other

useful weapons and tools to help him on the quest. Hermes gave him winged sandals that gave him the ability to fly. Hades' gift was a helmet that rendered the wearer invisible. This meant Perseus could get close to the Gorgons without being seen.

From Zeus, Perseus got a sword that he could use to slay Medusa. But it was Athena's gift that would be the most useful. The mortal Gorgon could not be defeated by the heroes who went before Perseus, and this was because the minute they saw her, they got turned to stone. To help Perseus, Athena lent him her shield, which had a mirror-like surface.

With all his gifts in hand, Perseus traveled to the cave of the Gorgons. There he found the statues of the fallen heroes who had tried to kill Medusa. They were turned into stone just by looking into Medusa's eyes, reminders of the peril that Perseus was about to face. Perseus used Athena's shield to find the Gorgons. Since it was safe to look at Medusa's reflection, Perseus used the shiny inside of his shield as a mirror to guide him as he walked carefully towards the Gorgons' cave. With the utmost caution, he looked inside and saw Medusa and her sisters sleeping.

Once he saw the reflection of the Gorgons on the shield, he quietly backed into the cave, taking care not to turn around. His steps were made lighter by Hermes' sandals, so Medusa and her sisters did not hear him come close.

Like a flash, Perseus ran inside the cave. He took his sword of adamant and chopped off Medusa's head. The hair of snakes still writhing, Perseus stuffed the head into his bag. From the bleeding neck of the dead Gorgon leaped out Pegasus, a great, winged horse, and Chrysaor, a beautiful young man. Pegasus and Chrysaor were the children of Medusa by Poseidon. They were born when Perseus killed their mother.

Stories say that drops of Medusa's blood fell on the Libyan region and immediately turned to snakes. These drops were also where the vipers that killed the Argonaut Mospus were born.

Once the deed was done, Perseus put on the helm of invisibility he had from Hades. When the Gorgons realized Medusa was dead, they tried to chase him, but because he was wearing the magical hat Hades gave him, they could not see him and thus could not catch him.

Caravaggio - *Medusa* - 1597

While Perseus had successfully killed Medusa, her power was far from gone. Her severed head could still turn people to stone, so it was a dangerous weapon to have. The young hero put it in the magic bag that he had gotten from the Hesperides.

Perseus and Andromeda

On his journey home, Perseus headed towards Ethiopia, where King Cepheus and Queen Cassiopeia ruled. Now, Cassiopeia and Cepheus had a daughter of astonishing beauty, whose name was Andromeda. Cassiopeia boasted that Andromeda was more beautiful even than the most beautiful of the Nereids, the nymphs of the sea.

Nereids were sea nymphs known for their kindness and beauty. They were the daughters of Nereus, a sea god known as "the old man of the sea". They also often accompanied Poseidon, the god of the sea, and could be friendly and helpful to the sailors they favored. But they could also be destructive, as they showed with Andromeda and Cassiopeia.

Cassiopeia's boast enraged Poseidon, for his wife, Amphitrite, was herself a Nereid. The mortal Queen had dared compare the beauty of her daughter to that of Poseidon's wife. Therefore, Poseidon commanded a great flood and sent a huge sea serpent to ravage the land all about. Cepheus went to the Oracle of Ammon to find out what to do.

The oracle had advised king Cepheus that if he sacrificed his daughter Andromeda to the serpent, Poseidon would be appeased and would relent on the curse. Cepheus and Cassiopeia were horrified by this, but the oracle had no further advice for them. Sacrificing Andromeda was the only way. Cepheus and Cassiopeia, therefore, took Andromeda and chained her to a rock beside the seashore. With many tears, they bid their beautiful daughter goodbye and then left her to her fate.

Flying with his winged sandals, Perseus approached Ethiopia's coast, where he saw beautiful Andromeda chained to the rock. Perseus then released her but she did not seem happy. Perseus asked her what was wrong and Andromeda explained she was there as a sacrifice to Poseidon, that he might stop flooding the land and sending his monster to eat the people and their livestock, and now that she had escaped, the sacrifice would not be valid anymore.

Perseus listened to Andromeda and felt pity and love for her. He told her he would help save the Ethiopians from the monster and save her too. He instructed her that once the monster appeared, she must keep her eyes closed and not look at any cost. Andromeda promised to do as he asked.

Perseus hid behind the rock and waited. Soon enough, the sea began to roil, and the waves began to rise: the monster was coming. But Perseus held fast. He waited until the monster was almost close enough to snatch Andromeda in its jaws, and then using his winged sandals, he flew in between the princess and the beast. He plunged his hand into his special bag and drew out the head of Medusa. Being careful not to look at it himself, Perseus showed it to the sea serpent.

André van Loo - *Perseus and Andromeda* - 1735

Being only a beast, the serpent did not have Perseus' wisdom and looked directly at the head. Even though Medusa was dead, her horror was still such that whatever looked at her turned to stone, and the sea monster was no different. The beast shuddered once and then fell into the water with a mighty splash. It sank to the bottom, a dead lump of monster-shaped stone.

Perseus freed Andromeda, but she did not escape the sacrifice, so Poseidon was pleased. When Perseus brought her back to her baffled and exultant parents, Andromeda explained what Perseus had done, and the king and queen offered him Andromeda's hand in marriage. Perseus gladly accepted, and soon he and the princess were wed. Perseus and Andromeda headed back to his birthplace in Argos as man and wife.

Back to Seriphos

Perseus then continued his journey back home, but before he got back to Seriphos, he passed by Atlas, who stood with the sky on his shoulders. When the titan tried to attack him, the brave hero took out Medusa's head again. Despite already being dead, the Gorgon's stare turned the titan to stone, thus creating the Atlas Mountains.

Edward Burne-Jones - *Atlas Turned to Stone* - 1878

Finally, after a long and eventful quest, Perseus was home. He found out that his mother was holed up in a temple hiding from King Polydectes, who still chased her. Perseus vowed that Polydectes would molest Danae no more, so he went into the throne room and said, "Behold, Polydectes, here is the gift I promised!"

Perseus then took Medusa's head out of the bag and showed it to Polydectes, who immediately turned into stone. With Polydectes gone, Perseus gave the throne of Seriphus to Dictys, as thanks for sheltering himself and his mother.

Homecoming

Acrisius learned that Perseus was on his way home. Acrisius was still worried about the prophecy that Danae's son would kill him, so he left Argos and went into exile in Thessaly. But this didn't save poor, greedy Acrisius. He decided to attend the funeral games that the king of Thessaly was holding after his father's death. Unbeknownst to Acrisius, Perseus was among the competitors at throwing the discus. When it was Perseus' turn, he gave the discus a mighty throw, but it went astray and veered into the crowd where it struck Acrisius on the head, killing him instantly. Thus, the prophecy was fulfilled.

Although Perseus was now heir to the throne, he didn't want to become king by having killed Acrisius, so he gave Argos to Megapenthes, the son of Acrisius' brother Proetus. In exchange, Megapenthes gave Perseus the throne of Tiryns. Megapenthes also renounced any right to take revenge on Perseus for the death of his uncle.

When all his deeds were done and his throne secured, Perseus returned all the magical items he had received from the gods, with many thanks to their owners. He gave Medusa's head as a special gift to Athena, who took it and fixed it into Zeus' aegis, which she carried from time to time.

Perseus and Andromeda ruled wisely and well for the rest of their days, and when they died, Athena set them as constellations in the heavens after Cepheus and Cassiopeia, and then to the great Pegasus, the winged horse of the gods.

The Aegis of Zeus was often described in ancient times as a kind of shawl or wrap. Many representations of Athena show her wearing this, with the head of Medusa prominently displayed on it. Today, we still use the phrase "under the aegis" to indicate protection or legitimacy because Zeus' aegis symbolizes his royal power. Athena might then wield as his proxy when she wore the aegis.

Benvenuto Cellini - *Perseus with the Head of Medusa* - 1554

ATHENA, GODDESS OF WISDOM AND WAR

Benvenuto Tisi da Garofalo - *Athena and Poseidon Battle for the Control of Athens* - 1512

An extraordinary birth

We already had a quick mention of Athena's birth, but let's see this out of the ordinary moment a little more in-depth before discovering more about the wise Zeus' daughter.

After Zeus had overthrown his father, Cronus, and become king of the gods, he found out one day that he and Metis, a wise and beautiful Titaness he was dating at the time, were going to have a baby.

Then Zeus heard a prophecy that if Metis had a son, he would overthrow Zeus, just like Zeus had overthrown Cronus. And Zeus didn't really like the idea.

After much consideration, he made a decision. He went to Metis and told her that he wanted to play a game. "Let's see who can become the smallest animal," he said. Metis agreed and turned herself into a shrinking and shrinking series of creatures: a fox, a bird, a mouse. When she became a fly, Zeus took the form of a frog and swallowed her.

Months after, while at home on Mount Olympus, Zeus got a massive headache. He felt like his head was going to split in half. When he couldn't take it anymore, he summoned his son Hephaestus, the blacksmith god, and asked him to break open his skull in hopes of relieving the pain.

Hephaestus swung his ax right down on his father's head, making a sound like rocks clashing against each other. A shadowy figure sprang from the wound, opening Zeus's skull in two. Now, that's a splitting headache. Hephaestus dropped his ax and stepped back, as the other Olympians, staring in disbelief.

With the mysterious figure, dark clouds went out from Zeus' skull covering the sky as if it were night. When the sky brightened again, they could see that the figure was not a baby girl or boy, but a woman. She wore a full suit of armor and her eyes were as gray and strong as the storm that had just passed. In one hand, she held a spear, in the other a shield. Her mother, Metis, had crafted all of this from the inside of Zeus's head.

She was Athena, an extraordinary goddess, born of extraordinary birth. From the moment of her birth, Athena was fully formed. She didn't need to grow up the way people usually do: she was already who she was meant to be. She never wanted to marry; she had so much to accomplish that she didn't have time for marriage. Naturally, being born holding weaponry she soon became the goddess of war. She also became the goddess of wisdom, often accompanied by an owl, which since then is a symbol of wisdom.

The foundation of Athens

One day, looking down from Mount Olympus, Athena noticed a hilly city. It was beautiful and lively, and she immediately knew that she wanted it for herself. Without much thought, she went down there from the mountain to stake her claim.

Right after she arrived, she heard a loud noise behind her. She turned around to see what it was about and saw Poseidon, sea god, and goddess' uncle, brandishing his enormous trident, with kelp tangled in his long hair.

She was taken aback and asked him what he was doing there, and Poseidon, a little startled himself, asked her the same question. Once they had the time to answer each other they realized that they went there at the same time for the same reason: taking the city.

Then they started arguing about who should get the city. Athena claimed that should have been her, because she arrived before the God of the sea, and because she thought she could have been more beneficial for the people of that city than Poseidon could.

On the other hand, Poseidon wouldn't give up and tried to assert his authority as one of the oldest Olympians, brother of Zeus, and the mighty ruler of the vast oceans and everything in them.

They continued to argue until it became clear that they would never agree. Then they decided to settle the matter with a contest and summoned the city's king to act as judge. The contest rules were simple: whoever came up with the most useful gift for the city would be the winner.

Poseidon went first. He slammed the base of his trident on the ground. Cracks formed where the trident struck, then widened until a jet of water burst forth and reached toward the sky. As the water spray lost its strength, it sank to the ground and pooled into a saltwater spring.

Then it was Athena's turn. Poseidon was a powerful god, as he had just shown, and he was her uncle too. Still, Athena refused to let him intimidate her. She gently tapped one of the cracks left by the trident with her spear. A sprout sprang out of the dirt and immediately started to grow incredibly quickly as if an invisible force were pulling it from above. Right after, an olive tree stood before them, as majestic, stout, and robust as it had been there forever.

It wasn't that tough of a call to decide the winner. Poseidon's spring was nice but filled with water too salty to drink or to be of some use for the plants. Athena's tree was far more useful. People could eat olives or press them to make oil. They could even use the wood from the trunk. The king of the city declared Athena the winner. She became the patron goddess and protectress of the city, which named itself "Athens" after her. Athens became a big and important city and today it is still the capital of Greece.

Athens was a credit to Athena, who had always been an extremely proud goddess. In spite of her great wisdom, sometimes Athena would push her pride a little too far. We may say, with all due respect, that perhaps she was a little touchy, a tiny bit too susceptible to offenses. The most famous example of this aspect of Athena's character is the story of a Lydian girl named Arachne.

Athena and Arachne

Arachne was a beautiful woman from humble and poor beginnings that had a great talent in weaving. Everyone was amazed at her work: true, pure talent. With just a few modest tools and some wool, she would create stunning artwork. The images she created with the wool seemed to come to life on the fabric and jump off it.

Nymphs and mortals alike came from all over to see her working skillfully across the fabric. Watching Arachne weave was a sight in itself, with her fingers dancing light while creating wonderful pieces of fabric. Arachne had learned to weave from the best: Athena herself.

Before long, Arachne became convinced that she was better than anyone, better even than Athena. The student had become the teacher. At first, Arachne kept that prideful thought to herself. But after a while, she began to brag and started telling the people who came to watch her that if she were given a chance she could beat Athena in a weaving contest. Pretty soon, the entire city was talking about that girl whose weaving surpassed a goddess'.

The word spread far and wide pretty quickly until it reached Mount Olympus and lodged itself in Athena's ear, making her increasingly annoyed. Finally, she felt that she had no choice but to confront Arachne.

When Athena arrived in Lydia, Arachne was at her loom, surrounded by a group of people that admired her work in reverent silence, as if they were watching a sacred ritual. Athena grew more irritated than ever. She decided to set a trap. She dyed gray some strands in her hair, carved wrinkles on her forehead, and made herself shaky and small. When she was finished, nobody could have guessed that she was a goddess and not a small old lady.

Athena worked her way through the crowd until she was standing right after Arachne. She tapped the girl on the shoulder. "Listen to the advice of an old woman, for there is wisdom in age," Athena told Arachne. "You may call yourself the best weaver among mortals, but you must not claim to be superior to a goddess. Apologize to Athena right now, and I am sure she will forgive you."

Arachne wrinkled her nose. She told the old lady that she didn't ask her for advice and that if telling that she was a better weaver than Athena was such a wrong claim then why Athena herself did not show up and accepted the challenge?

At that point Athena revealed herself. "She has".

The whole crowd gasped in surprise. Arachne was terrified and realized that she couldn't escape that challenge she bragged to want. But she did her best not to show her feelings. Just like Athena, Arachne was too proud to retreat at that point. So the two of them sat down at their looms, each determined to create a workpiece that would surpass the other's.

Athena loved showing off in front of an audience, and competition made her so excited. And she couldn't wait to finally put that presumptuous girl in her place.

Tintoretto - *Athena and Arachne* - 1579

The two competitors completed their handcraft quickly, and the whole audience gathered around to see the results. Athena's work was perfect. The stitches were so flawless that the images looked more like drawings than like texture. The tapestry showed her divine family performing all kinds of feats, and Athena couldn't resist scratching the itch of adding some scenes of the gods punishing human arrogance. Then she surrounded it off with an ornament of olive leaves.

Murmurs of admiration went up from the audience at the sight of Athena's tapestry. Then they turned to look at what Arachne had done.

Arachne's tapestry was flawless just like the Goddess' one. It was possibly the best one she had ever made. But being the technical quality of the two works equally perfect, what was absolutely different was the content of the image. In one scene, Zeus was seducing Europa by pretending to be a snowy bull. In another, Poseidon was turning into a bird to deceive Medusa. In yet another, Athena's half-brothers Apollo and Dionysus were also dressing up to trick women. Every part of Arachne's weaving depicted different ways that the gods, and particularly Zeus, had misled and abused mortals, tricking and seducing many women.

Athena was equally shocked by the anger for the insolent offense to the Gods and the envy for the flawless quality of the weaver.

Athena was not afraid of the other Olympians. After all, she entered this world by her father's head opened by an ax. And she had won the city of Athens besting her uncle in a public contest. But gazing upon Arachne's tapestry, she realized that she could not stand a human not showing fear to the Gods. She could not allow Arachne to go unpunished for making a fool out of her family.

Athena took up her spear and sliced Arachne's tapestry into strips. Then she lifted the wooden spindle from Arachne's loom and began to whack her on the head.

Out of humiliation, Arachne hanged herself on a nearby tree. Only then Athena felt pity for the poor girl whose extraordinary talent, the only thing of value that she owned, had led to her end. So she walked over to Arachne and touched her with a magical herb.

The rope from which Arachne hung turned into a fine thread of silk. The girl's body shrank, and her arms and legs doubled in number. Arachne was now a spider, allowed to continue beyond death the work she has such an amazing talent for.

And this is why spiders belong to the family of animals called arachnids.

Gustav Klimt - *Pallas Athena* - 1898

THE TWELVE LABORS OF HERACLES

Jean Baptiste Marie Pierre - *Diomedes King of Thrace Killed by Hercules and Devoured by his own Horses* - 1742

Heracles, more commonly known today under his Roman name Hercules, was arguably the greatest hero of Greek mythology. He certainly was, and still is the most famous. His feats can be compared to others like Perseus and Theseus, but the twelve labors that Heracles had to overcome reached the higher level of fame, to the point that still today in Europe "the twelve labors" is a way of saying that indicates something exhausting one have to confront. The origin of his labors was a punishment laid upon him by the gods. Heracles was prone to fits of madness, and it was during one of such flashes of rage that Heracles slew not only his brother's children but his own too.

Heracles' punishment for his horrible crime was to serve the king of Argos, Eurystheus. Like Heracles' parents, this king was descended from the hero Perseus. As part of his atonement for his misdeeds, Heracles was ordered to complete ten labors over ten years.

Yes, ten. How these became twelve we'll discover soon. These labors were considered impossible, as they certainly would have been for an ordinary man. Heracles though was no ordinary man, and despite the virtual impossibility of the tasks, he managed to carry them all out, making him eternally famous as the greatest and strongest of men (though he technically was a demigod since he was the son of Zeus).

Mosaic in the National Archeological Museum of Spain of Madrid - *The Twelve Labors of Heracles* - 3rd Century AD

His first task was to overcome the Nemean lion, and this is why Heracles is often depicted wearing a lion's skin.

First Labor: The Nemean Lion

The first labor involved the beating of a lion known as the Nemean lion. This lion was named after Nemea, a place near Corinth where the lion lived. The lion ravaged the area of Nemea, and since its fur was impenetrable by the weapons of humans it was considered undefeatable.

The Nemean lion was an enormous creature who was the offspring of Selene, the goddess of the Moon. The Nemean lived in a cave that has two entrances. Heracles tried many times to kill the lion by shooting arrows, but in vain, because of its impenetrable skin. But Heracles did not lose heart and came up with an idea. He would block one of the entrances, allowing only one escape route. Then, Heracles fought the lion and strangled it with his bare hands, much as he did to the serpents in his crib when he was a baby.

Pieter Paul Rubens - *Heracles and the Nemean Lion* - 1639

Second Labor: The Hydra Of Lerna

The Hydra of Lerna was a monstrous serpent with nine heads. Two heads regrew each time one was lopped off, making the hydra apparently unbeatable. It would rise up from the swamp near Lerna and terrorize the countryside. In this labor, Heracles was accompanied by his nephew Iolaus, who would be with him for many of the labors. Heracles lured the creature from the safety of its den by shooting flaming arrows at it. Once the hydra emerged,

Heracles seized it and attacked its many heads, but as soon as he smashed one head, two more would burst forth in its place. Then Iolaus came in helping Heracles by burning the stumps of the hydra's heads after Heracles lopped them off to prevent the heads from growing back.

John Singer Sargent - *Hercules and the Hydra* - 1921

Eurystheus though, said that since Iolaus had helped his uncle, this labor would not count for the ten.

Third Labor: The Hind Of Ceryneia

The earlier labors of Heracles seem to involve the beating of vicious and tremendous creatures, which may seem just an exercise in brute strength on the part of the Theban hero. The Hind of Ceryneia was so-called because it lived in Ceryneia, a city in Arcadia, forested land in the Peloponnese peninsula center. This was a large peninsula that covered the southern half of Greece. On this peninsula other than Ceryneia were located several cities, including Sparta, Argos, and Elis. The main cities of Arcadia were called Tegea and Mantinea.

The Hind of Ceryneia was a beautiful animal, a deer and for once the creature was not terrorizing anyone. The task of Heracles was to capture this hind. Slaying it might have angered the goddess Artemis, so to spare the hero this goddess's wrath the task was to merely capture the creature. The deer ran very swiftly, making it difficult for the hero to capture it. It was said to have feet made of bronze and antlers the color of gold metal.

After more than a year, when the deer had become weary with the chase, it looked for a place to rest on a mountain called Artemisius, and then headed to the river Ladon. Realizing that the deer was about to get away, Heracles shot it and wound it just as it was about to cross the stream. On his way back, with the deer on his shoulders, Heracles was met by Artemis and Apollo.

The goddess was very angry with Heracles for trying to kill her sacred animal, and she was about to take the deer away from him, and surely she would have punished him, but Heracles told her the truth. He told her that he had to obey the oracle and do the labors Eurystheus had given him and that he did not intend to kill the hind but just wound it in order to be able to capture it. Artemis accepted the explanation, let go of her anger, and healed the deer's wound. Heracles took the hind to Eurystheus unharmed.

Fourth Labor: The Wild Boar Of Erymanthus

For the fourth labor, Eurystheus ordered Heracles to bring him the Erymanthian boar alive. The beast was called the Erymanthian boar because it lived on a mountain called Erymanthus. Every day the boar would come down from his lair on the mountain, attacking men and animals all over the countryside and destroying everything in its path.

Antonio Tempesta - *Hercules and the Boar of Erymanthus* - 1608

At the time of this labor, the fields of the wild boar of Erymanthus were covered with snow. Heracles hunted the animal through fields that were covered inches deep with snow. Heracles could hear the beast snorting and stomping as it prowled for something to eat. Heracles chased the boar shouting as loud as he could. The boar, frightened and out of breath, hid in a thicket. Heracles with his spear made the animal go into a deep patch of snow. Hampered by the snow the boar could not run anymore, and Heracles captured it with a net and carried it to Eurystheus in Mycenae.

Fifth Labor: The Augean Stables

The fifth step of Heracles' labors is one of the more interesting ones. Heracles' task was to clean the stables of King Augeus. Heracles only had one day to accomplish this labor. Augeus was king of Elis, which was located on the Western end of the Peloponnesus Greek region where the Olympic Games would soon be held.

King Augeas owned more cattle than anyone in Greece. He was very rich, and he had many herds of cows, bulls, goats, sheep, and horses. And therefore his stable was huge, as huge was the amount of... organic material to get rid of, let's say.

Since the unpleasant job had to be done, Heracles thought to get a little gain out of it, so without telling anything about Eurystheus' order, he told Augeas that he would clean out the stables in one day if Augeas would give him a tenth of his cattle. The offer seemed too good to be true and so Augeas took it.

For this task, Heracles did not lay upon his brute force or physical abilities but on his intellect and smartness. First, he tore a big opening in the wall of the cattle-yard where the stables were, then he made a similar opening on the opposite wall of the yard. Next, he turned the course of two rivers that flowed nearby into the yard. The rivers rushed through the first hole in the wall of the yard and flowed through the stables, flushing all the mess out the hole in the wall on the other side of the yard.

At first, Augeas did not want to pay Heracles and denied that he had even promised to pay a reward. They took the matter in front of a judge that after the deposition of Augeas' son that swore that his father had agreed to give Heracles a reward, ordered that the compensation would be paid. Good news for Heracles. The bad news, though, was that Eurystheus said that this labor didn't count too, since Heracles got paid for it.

And that's how the ten labors became twelve.

Sixth Labor: The Stymphalian Birds

There is something truly frightening about birds, and the Stymphalian birds were no exception. These birds' claws, beaks, and wings were made of this metal alloy.

The Stymphalian Birds had an appetite for the human flesh. These birds were so numerous that their mass obscured the sun when they all took flight together. They settled on the trees near a deep lake near the town of

Stymphalos. So Heracles' first challenge was to find a way to frighten them out of their hiding place. The second issue was then to make them never come back to the lands they ravaged.

Gustave Moreau - *Hercules and the Stymphalian Birds* - 1872

The goddess Athena came to his aid, providing a pair of bronze krotala, noisemaking clappers similar to castanets. These noisemakers had been made by the immortal craftsman, Hephaestus, the god of the forge, that you may remember for having forged Pandora and participated in the birth of Athena herself by splitting Zeus' head in two with his ax. Heracles managed to frighten the birds by using the giant bronze rattle to create a horrible noise and then shot them with bow and arrow, or according to some sources with a slingshot, as they took flight so that the birds that were not killed were still scared enough not to ever come back.

The healing powers attributed to Heracles among many others were associated with his feat in this labor. Since Heracles healed the land by getting rid of the infesting birds that plagued it, a wider healing power extended to humans too was attributed to him in the popular myth.

Seventh Labor: The Cretan Bull

Crete was a land famous for bulls. The Cretans were known for the sport of bull-leaping, in which contestants grabbed the horns of a bull and were thrown over its back. So they weren't easily scared by bulls. At the time of this labor, though, a particularly strong and violent bull was terrorizing the island. Heracles's task was to capture this bull and return with it to mainland Greece.

This was maybe one of the easiest tasks for Heracles, who didn't have a hard time wrestling and capturing the bull and bringing it back to Eurystheus. But apparently, Eurystheus was more interested in giving Heracles challenging tasks than in taking out of circulation the dangerous bull. So he let the bull go free. It wandered around Greece, terrorizing the people, and ended up in Marathon, a city near Athens, where sometime after it was killed by Theseus during the quest for the minotaur, of which we shall read later.

Eighth Labor: The Horses Of Diomedes

Diomedes was the king of a Thracian tribe called the Bistones. His horses were mares that Diomedes fed with human flesh. Even though flesh-eating monsters were a common trope in Greek legend, horses that fed on human flesh are kind of unique. Heracles' task was to get these mares and bring them to Eurystheus.

Heracles sailed with a band of volunteers across the Aegean to Bistonia. There he and his companions overpowered the grooms who were tending the horses and drove the animals to the sea. But by the time they got there, the Bistones had realized what had happened and sent a band of soldiers to get back the animals.

Heracles fought the Bistones, killed Diomedes, and put the others to flight. He took the mares back to Eurystheus, but, as he did for the Cretan Bull, the king of Argus set them free. The mares wandered around and eventually, they arrived at Mount Olympos, the home of the gods, where they were eaten by wild beasts.

Ninth Labor: The Girdle Of The Amazon

Hippolyta was the most famous queen of the Amazons, a tribe of warrior women. Heracles's task here was to obtain the girdle of Hippolyta. It was a leather belt that had been given to her by Ares, the god of war, in recognition of being the best warrior of all the Amazons. King Eurystheus wanted to use this Amazonian girdle as a gift for his daughter.

Heracles sailed to the Amazons' land with a group of soldiers, and once he was there he asked to talk to Hyppolite. He told her about his quest and the labors he was into, and she agreed to give him the girdle. According to one version of the story, Hippolyta fell in love with Heracles and this was the reason for her decision.

This seemed too easy to be true. and in fact, the quest was not over yet. Hera was not pleased with what was happening, so she disguised herself as an Amazon and got to the Amazons. Hera told the warriors that Heracles had tricked Hyppolite and he was trying to kidnap her. Fomented by Hera's words, the Amazons hurried to Heracles' ship. When Heracles saw the warrior women coming in full armor and battle formation, he grabbed Hippolyta's girdle (in the "romantic" version gave her a quick kiss), and sailed away, leaving the queen of Amazons behind on the shore.

Tenth Labor: Geryon's Cattle

Geryon was the name of a monster with three heads. He was the son of Chrysaor and Callirrhoe. Chrysaor, as you may remember, was the giant with the golden sword that had sprung from the body of the gorgon Medusa after Perseus beheaded her. Unlike other monsters, however, Geryon kept a herd of cattle for which he was quite famous in Greece. Eurystheus envied the multi-headed monster his cattle, and he assigned to Heracles the labor of getting him these cattle.

Heracles was expected to steal the cattle, which he did deftly. Just as he was escaping with the cattle, Geryon attacked him. Heracles fought with him and shot him dead with his arrows. The stealing was not the hardest part of this mission. During the journey back Heracles had to fight on many circumstances not to be robbed in its turn, and on a few occasions, he had to make some detour to get back part of the cattle that had managed to escape.

After a long journey, he brought the cattle of Geryon to Eurystheus, who sacrificed the herd to Hera.

Eleventh Labor: The Apples Of The Hesperides

The Hesperides were the daughters of Atlas. Atlas was the Titan who was damned to carry the earth and the sky on his shoulders for leading the Titans against the Olympians. The golden apples of the Hesperides were the property of Hera, wife of Zeus. It was the job of a dragon called Ladon to guard the apples against anyone who might try to take them.

Giovanni Antonio Pellegrini - *Heracles in the Garden of the Hesperides* - 1718

The quest for the apples was long and full of difficulties.

On his journey, Heracles had to fight with Kyknos, the son

of the war god, Ares, and then the sea-god Nereus, who

knew the garden's secret location of the apples. Once he defeated Nereus Heracles got the information he needed. Still, on the way to the secret place he had to defeat also Antaeus and Busiris, two sons of the sea god, Poseidon.

Then Heracles came to the rock on Mount Caucasus where, as we know, Prometheus was chained with a monstrous eagle coming every day to eat his liver. This went on for 30 years, until Heracles, on his quest for the divine apples, arrived there and killed the eagle. In gratitude, Prometheus told Heracles the secret to getting the apples. The only one who could make it was Atlas, so he should have found the way to talk the Titan into going to get them for him.

Now, holding up the earth and the sky was not the work Atlas always has dreamed of. On the contrary, he hated it. So when Heracles asked him to fetch the apples while he would get the burden from him, he agreed without even thinking about it. Then Atlas went to get the apples while Heracles was stuck in his place, with the weight of the world on his shoulders.

When Atlas returned with the golden apples, he offered Heracles to take them to Eurystheus himself and asked Heracles to stay there and hold the heavy load until he would be back. Heracles agreed but asked Atlas to take it back again, just for a moment, just the time to put something soft padding on his shoulders to better bear the weight of the sky and the earth. As incredible as it may sound it worked, and so Heracles picked up the apples and ran off.

This labor, like many others, ended up seeming more of Eurystheus having fun creating impossible tasks for the hero than asking him something he really wanted. That's right, because, since they belonged to the gods, Eurystheus could not keep the apples. So after all that trouble, he had to return them to Athena, who took them back to the garden at the northern edge of the world.

Twelfth Labor: The Theft Of Cerberus

The most dangerous labor of all was the twelfth and final one. Eurystheus ordered Heracles to go to Tartarus (the Underworld) and kidnap the beast called Cerberus (or Kerberos). Eurystheus wanted to be sure Heracles would never succeed.

Cerberus was the vicious hound that guarded the entrance to Tartarus. It was a three-headed dog with a serpent for a tail, and heads of snakes all over his back, whose job was to prevent alive people who were not meant to be there from getting into the underworld.

Heracles went to a place called Taenarum in Laconia. Through a deep rocky cave, Heracles arrived in the Underworld. During the path, he encountered monsters, heroes, and ghosts, then, finally, he found Hades and asked him for Cerberus. The god of the Underworld told Heracles that he could take Cerberus with him if he submitted the beast with nothing more than his own brute strength.

Johann Köler - *Heracles Removes Cerberus from the Gates of Hell* - 1855

So Heracles set off unarmed to find Cerberus and he found it near the gates of Acheron, one of the five rivers of the

Underworld. The hero threw his strong arms around the beast, grasping all three heads at once, and wrestled it into submission. The dragon in the tail of Cerberus bit Heracles, but that did not stop him. The beast had to submit to the force of the hero, and Heracles brought Cerberus to Eurystheus. Finally, of course, Cerberus was returned safely to Hades, where he got back guarding the gateway to the Underworld.

So the ten, plus two, labors of Heracles were done, and he was finally free to get back to his everyday hero life.

THE CHAINS OF PROMETHEUS

Gustave Moreau - *Prometheus* - 1868

We already met Prometheus, the wise Titan, but it is worth going deeper into his story, since among all the deities he was the one that loved humanity the most, to the point, as we know to sacrifice himself to give it a better life. By contrast, having assumed kingship among the immortals, Zeus did not have in high regard the human beings, the unhappy ones who live on the earth. In fact, he had decided to exterminate their seed and start another human race.

The only one to oppose this was Prometheus, and it was thanks to his intervention that the mortals were not wiped off the face of the earth.

Prometheus often went to earth to comfort human beings, who then still lived in a wild state, living in caves, Unaware of the most basic knowledge and time cycles.

Prometheus taught them to work wood, model bricks, and build houses. He showed them the basics of farming, and how to put oxen in a yoke to plow the fields. He built the first wagons and ships and donated them to humans. He taught them astronomy, and how to use the rhythm of the rising and setting of the sun and the stars, and the moon's cycles, to measure time and live accordingly to it. He also taught them to count and instructed them in writing to preserve the memory of events. He showed humanity the medicinal herbs and how to use them for mixtures in order to cure diseases. And he revealed to mortals the gifts hidden in the earth and the use of metals.

Jean-Simon Berthélemy - *Prometheus Creating Men in the Presence of Athena* - 1802

Other than all of this practical knowledge, Prometheus taught the different forms of divination, the dark omens, the prophetic encounters, and taught humanity how to interpret dreams. He showed how to draw auspices from the flights of birds of prey, instituted sacrifices to the gods, and taught to read the bowels of animals immolated on the altars.

In short, for the ancient Greeks, everything that men know comes from Prometheus. In some traditions he is even considered the creator of humanity.

At the time of the first Bronze Age, in the city of Mecone, a dispute was between men and gods. Prometheus, to deceive Zeus, offered to make a sacrifice to resolve the quarrel. He cut up a bull and divided it into two parts. He wrapped up the best parts and the intestines in the skin, and at the top, he placed the stomach, one of the worst parts. The second heap consisted of the bones hidden under a delectable layer of fat white.

Zeus rebuked him for having divided the parts in a very unfair way, and Prometheus, aware of the trick he had set, replied with a slight smile asking Zeus to choose one of the two heaps.

Zeus fell into the trap: he chose the tempting fat-covered heap, and as lifted it with both hands he became extremely angry in his heart seeing the white ox bones prepared to deceive him.

Since that day, on earth, men have burned above the altars the bones of the animals sacrificed to the gods, but they consumed the meat.

Until that day, life for humanity had been rather easy: they just got what they needed ready for them to use. But Zeus, offended by the deception of Prometheus, hid all means subsistence, and from that day, work and struggle for survival became part of everyone's life.

Until then, moreover, humans, unable to produce fire by themselves, used to get it from the trees struck by lightning. From that moment on, Zeus no longer sent lightning on earth, who remained cold and dark, with no more trace of the power of fire. Humans have got their meat with deception, but now they must eat it raw!

Pieter Paul Rubens - *Prometheus* - 1636

As the friend of men we know he was, Prometheus figured out a stratagem to steal the fire from the gods. In some versions of this story is taught he stole the flame directly from Zeus' home. According to others, he failed to reach the top of Mount Olympus, guarded by Bia and Kratos, personifications of force and strength other than Zeus personal bodyguards, and so he went to Lemnos' island where Hephaestos had his forge.

The Titan seized the fire's sparks and, hidden in a narthex cane, brought them to the mortals. Since then, our ancestors managed to preserve the flame and be able to warm themselves and cook their food, thanks to Prometheus who faced the gods' inevitable punishment to lighten the burden of human life on earth.

Zeus' revenge, of course, was not late to come. Prometheus was brought on the cliffs of Mount Caucasus. For the Greeks, the Caucasus mountains were the pillars of the world and represented the end of it.

According to some versions, Zeus tied Prometheus to a column, with indissoluble laces. Others say that Kratos and Bia dragged Prometheus to the place of his punishment and Hephaestus was commissioned to chain him to the rock. The latter is the most famous version, especially because of the many paintings depicting the Titan chained to the mountain.

Although Prometheus stole fire in his forge, Hephaestus was not happy to execute the order given by Zeus. For the god of fire was unbearable to commit such an act of violence. However, on the other hand, he dared not refuse the orders received by the supreme god.

Hephaestus knew that this punishment was the consequence of the Titan's love for humanity. He honored men as gods and this was against the divine law, but still, it was out of a form of love that Prometheus broke that law, and now faced his punishment. Hephaestus felt bad that he had to execute that punishment, however, he could do anything but do it.

Kratos and Bia, who were a little less sensitive than Hephaestus, insisted that he obey the order, and they remained there to make sure the work was carried out as it should and not influenced by Hephaestus' soft heart. The guardians locked iron rings around Prometheus' wrists and ankles, and chained his chest and waist with metal belts, nailing then the belts to the rocks, so that they could not be loose.

Carried out the sad task, Hephaestus left, while Kratos and Bia took one last look at Prometheus. Unlike the fire God, they were convinced that the punishment was well deserved, and they didn't miss the chance to let Prometheus know that.

After Zeus' two relentless bodyguards had moved away, Prometheus started moaning, invoking Divinities in all of their forms for them to look at the pain that was consuming him under the torture of an undeserved divine punishment that was intended to last for eternity. The only reason for his punishment was his affection for mortals, this was the reason why he stole the fire, and he shouted against this fate he could not accept in silence.

And still, Zeus was not satisfied with such an atrocious punishment. Keeping Prometheus chained to the mountain for eternity was not enough for the angry king of Gods, so Zeus sent against him an eagle, daughter of Echidna and Typhon. Every day, the bird of prey descended on him and devoured pieces of his liver. At night, the liver of the immortal Prometheus grew back, so that he could stay alive and the torture might never end.

The intercession of other gods and titans had no effect. The lord of all gods did not show any mercy.

Prometheus, for his part, never accepted begging for mercy. On the contrary, he shouted to heaven that one day

Zeus would also be ousted from the throne if he joined in a wedding with a goddess who would generate a son stronger than him. Prometheus claimed to know the name of the goddess who could have given birth to such a powerful creature but never would have revealed it until Zeus had decided to free him from the unfair punishment.

Theodoor Rombouts - *Prometheus* - 1625

But this attempt to get free did not convince Zeus, still firm in his decision. And as we know, the liberation of the Titan did not occur for a long time, and when it did it wasn't out of the pity of Zeus but at the hands of Heracles.

ODYSSEUS AND THE TROJAN HORSE

Archeological Museum of Sperlonga - *Odysseus' Head* - 1st Century AC

Odysseus, also known under his roman name of Ulysses, is one of the most famous and important heroes of Greek mythology. To get an idea of the importance of this character in ancient Greece we can just consider that one of the most important, if not *the* most important, works of literature of the Greek epics, the Odyssey, is named after the Greek hero of which it tells the deeds.

Homer's Odyssey is one of the greatest and most famous works in the history of literature. The poem narrates the adventures of Odysseus by mixing historical reality with myths and legends. And of course, when we talk about Odysseus we can't help thinking about the Odyssey and Homer.

It is not easy to choose among the amazing stories the blind poet gave us about Odysseus. How he outsmarted the giant Cyclops Polyphemus, how he managed to listen to the sweet chant of the sirens without getting killed by it, the adventures with Circe who turned men into swine or other animals, the way he returned back home to rescue his faithful wife Penelope defeating her unwanted suitors, and the list would go on and on.

Giovanni Andrea Sirani - *Ulysses and Circe* - 1655

The adventures of Odysseus in the Odyssey would deserve a whole book just for them. Ok, such a book already exists, it is called the Odyssey, but ok, you know what I mean... Anyway, among all the stories about Odysseus, there is one that is very famous and that in the Odyssey is just mentioned in passing, This is the story of the Trojan horse and of how Odysseus was able to win with his smartness a war that the military force was struggling to conclude.

Despite being a war hero, Odysseus was not a bellicose guy yearning to build his name upon military achievements. On the contrary, when the war began, his wife had just given birth and he wanted to spend some time with his new child Telemachus. So, to avoid military service he tried the oldest trick in the book: pretending to be mentally unstable.

Then Odysseus went out into the fields and started sowing salt. The news spread that he had got a bit nutty and that he could not go to war. King Menelaus though, that knew Odysseus as a man of the utmost intelligence, was not convinced, and he wanted to check himself. So he went to the field Odysseus was seeding salt into and, while the latter was passing with his plow the king put the little Telemachus on the way. Odysseus changed his way not to kill his own son and so the king knew he was sane.

So Odysseus had to go to war. The war was long and grueling and had been on for ten solid years – the two sides had lost some of their best warriors and heroes. Both forces were tired but didn't know how to bring the war to an end. The more the war lingered, the more men the two sides would lose.

One day, Odysseus came up with a great idea that would end the long exhausting war for good. He for one had grown even more tired of a war he didn't want to take part in in the first place and wanted it to end. The plan was clever and would end the war if well executed.

Odysseus told his idea to the other Greek soldiers who saw that it was feasible, and they set to work on it.

First, they procured wood and started with the construction of a horse. It was an enormous horse of wood with a hollow interior. Once they were done building the horse, some soldiers were hidden inside. The wooden horse was then wheeled and placed in front of the city gates of Troy.

After leaving the horse at the city gates, all the Greek soldiers who weren't inside the horse, except one named Sinon, got into their ship and sailed to the nearby island of Tenedos. Sinon was left to execute an important task: to serve as the messenger of the Greeks.

So once the other Greek soldiers had sailed, Sinon went to the city gate and talked to the Trojans. The Trojans who saw the giant horse didn't know what it was and were quite curious about it. Sinon then told the Trojans that the wooden horse was intended as a gift to the gods from the Greeks to ensure their safe voyage home

He told them that the Greeks made the horse too big for the Trojans to move it into their city because with the horse in the city they would be invincible. The Trojans looked towards the sea and they didn't see the Greek ship. With the ship out of the port, the Trojans believed Sinon and thought that the war was over.

Cassandra, the prophetess of Athena, and Laocoon, one of Apollo's priests, had tried to warn the Trojans that the wooden horse was not a real gift for the gods. However, the people didn't believe the priest and the prophetess. Sinon's story sounded plausible and credible. Also, the Trojans had looked around and didn't find any Greek soldier. So, they just believed that the Greeks had withdrawn from the war.

The Trojans were extremely happy about the end of the war, and they also decided to bring the horse inside their city to get the protection of the gods and become invincible. There were huge feasts and celebrations throughout the night. Since the war had lasted for ten long years, the news of its end was worth celebrating.

Giovanni Domenico Tiepolo - *The Procession of Trojan Horse in Troy* - 1760

Meanwhile, the Greek soldiers, according to Odysseus' plan, while the Trojans were celebrating behind the city's locked walls, were sailing back from Tenedos into Troy during the night.

When the other Greeks had come back to Troy, the soldiers hidden in the wooden horse jumped out, attacked by surprise the Trojans, who were still celebrating, and opened the city gates. The entire Greek army got right into the city and massacred every Trojan and finally conquered Troy.

THESEUS AND THE MINOTAUR

George Frederic Watts - *The Minotaur* - 1885

Child of a human mother and a bull father, the Minotaur was one of the most dreaded beasts in ancient Greece. Living in a maze on Crete island, the Minotaur lay there waiting for a detainee to enter its abode. Then, once seized, the victim would be brutally torn and ate up by the vicious monster.

The Minotaur was brought into being by an offense toward the god Poseidon by the king of Crete, Minos. The ruler had implored Poseidon to send a white bull, as a sign to confirm him as the legitimate beneficiary to Crete's throne. Minos had vowed, upon its appearance, to sacrifice the bull to Poseidon, but later, enchanted by the bull's magnificence, Minos went back on his vow. In another version of this story, Minos would have sacrificed the new bull to Poseidon. However, once he received the white bull, he could not force himself to sacrifice it. He butchered another bull, thinking that the god would have been equally satisfied.

What is consistent in both versions is Poseidon's response to the king's fault. He caused Minos' better half, Queen Pasiphae, to experience passionate feelings for the bull. The sovereign yearned to make love with the monster. She ordered a famous Athenian artisan named Daedalus to manufacture her a wooden bovine, empty within.

The sovereign brought the artifact into the field where the bull lived, entered it, and the rest is best left to the reader's imagination. She got pregnant and, upon her deception, the Minotaur (or bull of Minos) was conceived.

Trying to make lemonade out of the lemons life gave him, Minos chose to use the Minotaur for his potential benefit. He charged Daedalus to design and build a jail wherein the Minotaur would be put, and any detainees would be compelled to confront it.

Androgeus, the son of Minos, was in Athens, contending in Panathenaic Games, an early archetype to the Olympics. He won each competition, maddening different contenders. These men murdered him. When Minos knew about this, he declared war on Athens.

Instead of a full-scale assault, Minos ordered that seven male virgins and seven female virgins chosen among noble citizens be offered to him in retribution for his son's death. The fourteen Athenians would have been given up to the Minotaur and confront it unarmed in the maze so that their choice was between getting devoured by the monster and getting lost forever in the labyrinth. And this kept going until it was the turn of Theseus, who volunteered to join the third group of the would-be victims, killed the monster, and led the others out of the Labyrinth.

Charles-Edouard Chaise - *Theseus VIctor of the Minotaur* - 1791

As the son of Aegeus, the King of Athens, or Poseidon, the god of seas, Theseus was meant to sit on the Athenian throne and had the divine forces on his side. When the time came, the third group of virgins was gathered, and he got together with them, vowing to cut down the horrible monster that had slaughtered those sent before him. Being grown up enough to recover his father's sword from underneath a rock (where Aegeus had put it when Theseus was born, waiting for him to be strong enough to pull up the rock), Aegeus had just one recommendation for his child. Should he succeed and get back, he should raise the white sail on its way back home to show his dad that he was alive. A black sail, instead, would have meant that he was dead.

At the point when Theseus showed up at Knossos, Crete's capital, he immediately grabbed Ariadne's attention, the daughter of King Minos. She became hopelessly enamored of him and went to Daedalus to discover some approach to enable the youngster to get back from his detainment in the maze. Daedalus provided her some advice and a ball of thread, so she could offer Theseus a path back to the passage of the labyrinth. She had one condition, however.

If Theseus would have succeeded, he would have married her. Theseus concurred.

The fourteen virgins were driven the following morning to the passageway to the maze and locked inside. With his ball of thread, Theseus would lead the way. He tied one end of the ball of string to the doorpost and bore the sword of Aegeus and advanced in obscurity through the maze, looking for the Minotaur.

Then he proceeded following Dedalus' directions to always go straight and never turn left or right and at some point, he came across the dozing Minotaur. Theseus ambushes the asleep animal, finding him napping. The two fought, the Minotaur using a hatchet, Theseus with a sword.

In the fight, however, Theseus rapidly has the high ground. He corners the Minotaur, kills and decapitates him. Yet he's not free and safe yet. The day is drawing nearer and, should Theseus and the virgins be gotten by ruler Minos, they will most likely be killed. He rapidly advances back through the maze, following the string that Ariadne had given him. Theseus and the others would escape at the end of the night. Before daybreak, Ariadne met Theseus on the Athenian's vessel, and the party set sail toward Athens.

Aegeus, Theseus' father, had gone to a cliff sitting above the ocean to discover his child's destiny. But Theseus had forgotten to raise the white sail, so when the boat was in view, Aegeus, believing his child to be dead, was distressed to such an extent that he committed suicide, casting himself over the bluff and dying. These waters would come to be known as the Aegean Sea, as it's called still today.

JASON AND THE GOLDEN FLEECE

Constantine Volanakis - *Argo* - 1894

Aeson was the heir to the throne of Iolcus, in Thessaly's kingdom, but his brother Pelias usurped it from him and had him imprisoned. Aeson had a son, Jason, and fearing Pelias would also kill the boy, he sent him away to Mount Pelion, to live with the Centaur Cheiron, a strange creature half-man half-horse. Centaur Cheiron became his tutor and Jason grew up to be a fine young man and a great warrior.

Pelias, still fearing he would lose his kingdom, approached the oracle at Delphi and was told to beware of a man with one sandal. The king couldn't know that this was part of a plan of Hera's revenge for many years before he prohibited the people of Iolcus from worshipping the goddess.

When he became twenty years old, Jason found out his true identity and set out to reclaim the throne and kingdom of Iolcus from his uncle.

During his journey to Iolcus Jason came across an old woman trying to cross over to the river Anauros. Jason helped the woman across but the current took away one of his sandals. Once the old woman was safe on the other bank, Jason continued on his journey unaware that the old lady he just had helped was no other than Hera in disguise.

Jason arrived at Iolcus during a celebration held in honor of Poseidon, sea god, and Pelias' father. Jason then met his uncle and asked for what was rightfully his: the throne of Thessalia. Uncle Pelias couldn't help noticing the one sandal worn by Jason, and he saw the prophecy close to be fulfilled. He needed to get rid of Jason, but he was afraid of fighting him, because of what the oracle told him. So he told Jason that he would get the throne when he brought back the Golden Fleece from Colchis.

The fleece had belonged to a magical ram and now nailed to a sacred tree guarded by two fire breathing, bronze-hoofed bulls, the Khalkouri, and a dragon, to prevent anyone from stealing it. So the plan of Pelias was to send Jason on an impossible mission and get rid of him for good.

Meet the Argonauts

Determined to win back the kingdom stolen from his father, Jason gathered warriors from throughout Greece to join him on his quest. This was sort of a Greek heroes dream team, that included Heracles, the two twins Castor and Pollux, the heroine Atalanta, and the musician Orpheus. Argos, who was famous for his skill as a shipwright, with the help of Goddess Athena who provided magic wood for the ship's prow, built Jason a vessel suitable to accommodate all these heroes. Jason decided to name his ship Argo after its builder and set sail in the gods' favor.

The crew encountered many adventures on its way to finding the Golden Fleece. On the island of Lemnos, they met a race of women who had horrible body odor due to a punishment from Aphrodite, whom they refused to worship. The stench had annoyed their husbands who had deserted them to this island, so the women had killed in revenge any male on the island. Some time had passed and, by the time Jason and the argonauts were there, the women were hungry for male companionship. The Argonauts stayed long enough to give the women a few children before leaving the island.

Then, when they were at Propontis, today Istanbul, replenishing their supplies, they were attacked by Gegenees, a tribe of six-armed Giants. Heracles handled them without difficulty.

On the next island, they met Phineus, a king who could predict the future. He was an old blind man that was cursed by Zeus who didn't like the idea of a mortal who could know the future. So Zeus had Harpies, bird-monsters with women heads, to take away Phineus's food whenever he tried to eat. The Harpies' torment left Phineus emaciated. Phineus agreed to tell the Argonauts what lay ahead as long as Jason and his friends would help him to get rid of the Harpies. The Argonauts defeated the monsters and got advice on navigating the Symplegades, rock cliffs that crushed any craft that would pass between them.

The Symplegades were two gigantic rocks that constantly clashed against each other. Thanks to Phineus' advice, when the Argonauts reached them, Jason sent a dove through the rocks first, which triggered the clashing. The Argonauts then rowed as fast as possible, threading through the rocks before they clashed again. Thus the Argo became the first vessel to pass the Symplegades safely.

When the Argo arrived in Colchis at last, King Aietes assigned Jason three difficult tasks to show he was worthy of the Golden Fleece. if he would succeed in all of the three the fleece would be his. As a first task, he had to plow a field with the king's fire-breathing oxen. Then he had to sow the teeth of a dragon into the field. If a dragon's teeth were sown in a field, they would sprout full-grown warriors so Jason had also to fight the army of warriors. Finally, he had to slay the dragon guarding the fleece. Jason completed the tasks with Medea's help, the sorceress daughter of the king, who had fallen in love with him.

Surprised at the hero's success, the king tried to kill Jason and the Argonauts. But they sailed away, bringing with them both Medea and the Golden Fleece. After many more adventures, they ran among others into Circe, the Sirens, and Talos the legendary giant of bronze, the crew arrived in Thessaly. Once there Jason handed the Golden Fleece to Pelias, unaware that his uncle had already killed his parents.

Jean François de Troy - *The Capture of the Golden Fleece* - 1746

Jason swore he would exact terrible revenge against Pelias and asked Medea to help him. Medea convinced Pelias' daughters that she had the power to restore their father's youth. She killed a ram, cut it into pieces, thrown it into a cauldron of boiling water, and then bring it back to life as a younger sheep. Pelias's daughters believed the sorceress' magic and killed their own father to make him youthful again.

Jason seized the throne thereafter but soon had to leave Iolcus because the citizens didn't want a sorceress as their queen. So Jason, after so many adventures to get the Golden Fleece and become a king, yielded the kingdom to Pelias' son, Acastus.

TALES OF ORIGINS

John William Waterhouse - *Persephone* - 1912

The tale about origins is one of the foundations of every mythology and religion (let's not forget that what we now call mythology was full-fledged religion back then). In fact, the explanation of the inexplicable is probably the main reason behind myths. How did it all begin? What are these flashing lights and menacing sounds in the sky? Why are some areas of this planet covered in plants and some others seem to be just sandboxes? Why are there so many different kinds of creatures?

Nowadays science has answered most of these questions, and still, this does not mean that there are no unanswered questions anymore, they have just changed. But in ancient times science was not able to give some answers, and where it was people were not always ready to understand them, so they needed something easier and more relatable. An electrostatic discharge with the instantaneous release of energy in form of light with consequent expansion of the air that causes a rumbling noise was not an understandable explanation for lightning and thunder, an angry Zeus screaming and throwing fire was.

We have already had an example of this kind of story in the tale of Athena and Arachne, where an angry and offended goddess turned an arrogant and talented in weaving girl into a spider. Below we have some other stories about the divine origin of natural phenomenons.

Persephone, Demeter And The Origin Of Winter

Persephone was the daughter of Zeus and Demeter. She became the queen of Tartarus through her abduction by Hades, the god of the underworld

One day the girl was out in the sunny world at springtime, running through the flowers and enjoying Nature. Her mother was the Goddess of the harvest, so she was grown up spending much of her time with her mother, loving everything that grew from the earth. Mother and daughter had a happy time together watching things grow and blossom and change with the seasons.

On that sunny day, Persephone was out picking lilies and violets and she thought how her mother would love a bouquet. As she wandered into a meadow, she heard a rumbling noise that seemed as the rocks were battling with the mountains, and suddenly the earth split open into an enormous cave before her.

As she looked up, she saw a dark figure riding a chariot pulled by four black stallions with red eyes and flaming nostrils.

Persephone began to run from the man, but he grabbed hold of her and pulled her into the chariot. He directed his chariot back into the cave as quickly as he had come out, and the earth closed up immediately behind them.

The chariot sped on, deeper and deeper through dark tunnels. Hades, the God of the Underworld, had captured her. He claimed to have fallen in love with her golden hair and sunny disposition and would never let her leave.

Walter Crane - *The Fate of Persephone-* 1877

As they crossed the River Styx, where the souls of the dead crossed over, they approached Hades' palace entrance, guarded by the monstrous Cerberus (remember the three-headed dog from the last labor of Heracles?)

As they entered the gate to the kingdom, Persephone was terrified at the thought of never being able to leave this ghostly place, for Hades told her she was to become Queen of the Underworld. Though she was given a gold crown with brilliant jewels to complement her sunny nature, her heart was cold as ice, and she would not eat or drink any of the offerings at her table.

Demeter had heard Persephone's screams as they echoed over the land, over the mountains, and across the seas as Hades took her to Tartaros. So she left Olympus and disguised herself as an old woman. She wandered the earth searching for her daughter for nine days.

When she, at last, came upon the very spot where Persephone was abducted, she encountered a man who told her he had heard the thundering noise and had seen the chariot spring from the cavern. He told her how the chariot's man grabbed the girl as she picked flowers and how the earth had closed up around them.

Demeter grew angry and sad because she knew that no one ever escaped the underworld, and no man could enter to rescue her lovely daughter. She was now doomed to confinement in the Underworld, and would never be able again to see the light of the sun or the flowers that she used to love so much.

Demeter was the goddess of the harvest, agriculture, and everything that grows from the earth. She was one thing with Nature, and this was going to be proved once again. Because of her grief trees ceased to bore fruit, every plant withered, and all the cattle died of starvation. It was a cold, cruel winter for humans.

Zeus knew that if Demeter would not rid herself of her anger and sadness, nature would perish, and with it humankind. He talked to Demeter and they made an agreement that he would take care to rescue Persephone, and Demeter would bring nature back to life. There was just one condition; Persephone must not have eaten the food of the dead.

He sent his messenger Hermes to the underworld to gain the release of the Goddess' daughter. Quite surprisingly, Hades would not discuss Zeus' wishes and agreed to let her go. But of course, he was not resigned to losing her. So, he told her that she was going to embark on a long journey back home and since she had not eaten for months, he offered her some pomegranate seeds for her journey. Of course, he knew that if she ate even one of the seeds, she would be bound to come back to him.

She ate four seeds then climbed onto Hermes' golden chariot. The messenger of the gods took her to Demeter's temple, where she was welcomed. Then Demeter asked her whether she had eaten any of the dead's food. When Persephone heard the details of the contract with Zeus, she wailed and cried.

Zeus took pity on her and decided to make a compromise. She would return to Tartaros in respect of the contract, but just for four months of each year, one month for each seed she had eaten, and that is why each year when Persephone is with Hades, the earth becomes cold and barren. When she returns to her mother in springtime, the earth springs again with grass, fruits, and flowers.

Phaeton and Helios

Helios, the sun god, had a youthful son, Phaeton, whom he adored. As the god of the sun, the job of Helios was basically to put the sun in a chariot and drive the chariot every day all along the sky.

One day, a mate of Phaethon laughed at his claim that he was the son of a god. Phaethon went to his mother in tears and told her what happened. His mother Clymene assured her son he was indeed the son of the god of the sun, Helios, and sent him to the palace of his father to get it confirmed directly from him.

Delighted and excited, Phaethon went to India, where was the palace of his father, from whom Helios was supposed to bring every day the gigantic ball of fire through the sky.

Phaethon told his father about the humiliation of being accused of illegitimacy. He begged Helios to recognize him as his son and assert beyond all doubt the legitimacy of his birth. Helios got moved and firmly affirmed his paternity and Phaethon's legitimacy as his own son. To seal his statement, he declared, in the front of all his attendants (the Day, the Month, the Year, the Hour, and also Spring, Summer, Autumn, and Winter), that he will grant his son any favor that he would ask him.

Phaeton, just as many boys wanting so badly to have a ride on their fathers' cars, asked Helios to allow him to drive the sun chariot.

Helios was worried by his son's irrational request. He tried to explain to Phaeton that He was the only one capable of driving the Chariot of the Sun, not even the mighty Zeus could, let alone a mere mortal.

No matter how he tried, his son stuck on his request. Now, a promise is a promise, and this applies even more to gods than to humans. Once the gods had promised a favor, they could not withdraw or deny it in any case. Helios tried it all to convince the rash Phaethon to withdraw his outrageous wish but in vain. The boy insisted that Helios kept his promise and the god of the Sun could do nothing but give in.

As soon as he took off, Phaethon realized that his father's advice was well-founded. It was impossible for him to control the fiery horses, and once they felt the weakness and inexperience of their young charioteer, they began to go wild. The Chariot of the Sun blazed a spiral gash in the sky which later became known as the Milky Way.

Godfried Maes - *Phaeton in the Chariot of the Sun God* - 1664

Then the out of control Chariot with the Sun began to fall low, hitting the earth, burning off the African continent and turning it into a desert, making the Ethiopian people black-skinned from the sunburns, and damaging the river Nile.

An angry Zeus, appalled by Phaeton's devastation, struck the boy with lightning and hurled his burning body into the Eridanos River, the Italian river now called Po. His sisters assembled on the river banks, where they were turned into poplar trees.

Phaeton was placed among the stars after his death and is seen as the constellation "Auriga," meaning "Charioteer" in Latin.

Cadmus and the Founding of Thebes

Cadmus was the son of Agenor and Telephassa, king and queen of Tyre. His sister Europa was abducted by Zeus. The king of the gods had been seduced by the beauty of Europa, so he did what he was used to when falling in love: kidnap her. So one day, when Europa and her fellow nymphs were gathering flowers, Zeus came to her disguised as a white bull.

Europa got close to the bull to stroke him, and the bull ran off with the princess of Tyre on his back. Then, swimming across the sea, he arrived in Crete where Europa realized that her abductor was none other than the chief of gods himself. In the following years, Europa gave birth to three sons from Zeus, married a king, and became the queen of Crete.

King Agenor was devastated at his daughter's disappearance. He gave his four sons, Cadmus, Phoenix, Cilix, and Thasus, the mission to find her, ordering them never to return without his beloved daughter. The queen Telephassa went on the quest with his sons too. They searched far and wide for Europa, but they weren't able to find her.

Faithful to their father's dispositions, the four brothers didn't return home. Once they gave up the quest Phoenix settled in a place later named Phoenicia after him, Cilix and Thasus settled in regions founding cities that were also named after them too: Cilicia, in Asia Minor and Thassos, on an island of the Aegean.

Cadmus settled in Thrace along with his mother Telephassa who soon died of grief at the loss of her daughter. After his mother's funeral Cadmus went on a pilgrimage to the oracle of Delphi to ask about his sister.

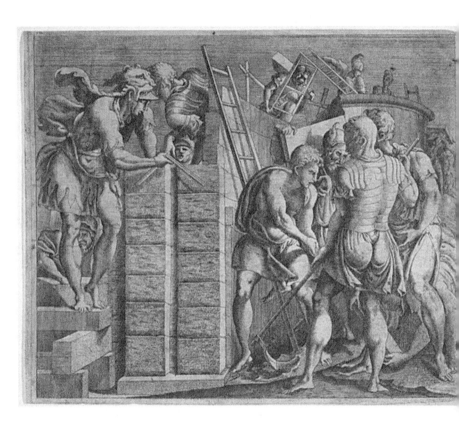

Francesco Primaticcio - *Cadmus Building Thebes-* 1543

The oracle told him to quit searching for Europa and instead to found a new city. He would have followed a cow he would meet outside the temple and found the city on the spot where the cow would lay down to rest. As predicted, Cadmus found a cow right out of the temple and followed it.

On that spot, Cadmus decided to found his city, and to start it under the best auspices, he thought to sacrifice the cow to Athena. There Thebes was born, the city from which the famous tales of Oedipus and Dionysus would come.

Also, Cadmus was famous to have brought the alphabet to Greece from Phoenicia.

Echo & Narcissus

As we now know, Zeus could not quit his old habit of cheating Hera with women and nymphs. Hera, for her part, could not quit being jealous and getting furious when she caught him (that, we must say, happened quite frequently).

John William Waterhouse - *Echo and Narcissus* - 1903

Well, at some point, Zeus had found that when he sneaked out on his wife to frolic with mountain nymphs, there was one of them that would be an involuntary sidekick to his affairs. That nymph was named Echo, and if Hera should go out on the mountain looking for her husband, she would keep the queen of the gods from finding out. How was that? Well, that was because Echo was a blabbermouth. A chatterbox. A tattletale. Or to put it in less funny words, she talked all the time.

So if Hera should be on his trail, Echo would be there, and while Echo chatted with Hera, Hera was distracted, and if

Hera was distracted, Zeus could do what he liked and get away with it. Of course, just as any other trick found by Zeus to cheat on his wife, it did not last that long. When Hera discovered Zeus' infidelities and realized that Echo was, even if just unwittingly, involved, that was bad news for the chatty nymph.

Hera cursed the blameless accomplice of her husband's affairs with the worst punishment: she took away the ability to talk, leaving her only the possibility to repeat others' words. Desperate at the idea of never again being able to speak for herself, Echo ran off into the forest and disappeared.

After some time of solitary despair, Echo encountered in the forest an incredibly handsome young man named Narcissus. Narcissus had a reputation for being proud, vain, and unfriendly, but she didn't know any of that. Everyone loved that young handsome man, but he believed none were good enough for his beauty. Echo, just as anybody else before her, fell in love with Narcissus and followed him through the woods, but was unable to speak to him because of Hera's curse.

Narcissus heard some steps and he called out, "Who's there?". She could only answer, "Who's there?". "Show yourself!" Narcissus demanded. "Show yourself!" answered the nymph.

Finally, she found the courage to show herself and dashed toward him. At the sight of yet another infatuated nymph, he pushed her and told her to go away. "Go away!" Narcissus said. "Go away!" Echo repeated and then burst into tears.

But Nemesis, the goddess of divine retribution, witnessed the scene, and when Narcissus stopped at a pond to drink, she carried out the vengeance on the cruel young man, cursing him to be unable to love anyone but himself. When he saw his reflection in the pond, Narcissus fell deeply in love with the handsome boy staring back at him. He then tried to touch him, but every time Narcissus reached for the reflection, the figure disappeared at his touch. So he just stayed there, staring at his own reflection. He didn't eat nor drink. He just gazed enraptured at his own face reflected in the water until he finally withered and died.

A white flower grew in the place where the young body died, and the nymphs named it "narcissus".

Artemis and Orion

Artemis was the virgin goddess of the hunt and was never much attracted by men. Just once she noticed one man for some time. He was a hunter too: the giant Orion, son of Poseidon. Modest and brave, Orion was also skillful at the hunt, but since he was aware that his skills were nothing compared to the hunter goddess Artemis', he never boasted about it.

One night on Crete's island the goddess saw an enormous shadow standing out against the night sky. He was Orion. Since they were both hunters she invited him to join her in a hunt, so they went on their hunting trip, talking and laughing as they traveled the wild places of Crete. Day after day, week after week, they kept hunting while telling each other stories and playfully competing against each other. They became best friends, and for a while, Artemis even thought about the possibility of marrying the mighty hunter.

Johann Heinrich Tischbein - *Diana and Orion* - 1764

But Apollo, her twin brother, grew jealous of this friendship. He had always been the most significant man in Artemis' life and intended to remain so. He was also worried that his sister's virginity was in danger. So Apollo sent a giant scorpion to attack Poseidon's son. The poisonous beast pushed Orion back towards the sea until he had no choice but to dive in. Relentless, the scorpion chased Orion into the sea too.

Then Apollo told his sister that an evil man had just raped one of her devotees and was now trying to swim away from the island. The goddess ran to the seashore and shot an arrow toward the escaping rapist. Artemis was the goddess of the hunt, and she never missed a shot. Unfortunately, she did not miss that one either, and the arrow hit its target. But then Artemis felt that something wasn't right seeing the relieved reaction of her brother. She immediately dived into the sea and swam out to see whom she had just killed and found out he was Orion, her best friend, who might have been her lover.

In her grief, Artemis asked Zeus to place Orion in the stars, so they would be able to keep hunting together at night. Zeus was moved by the sad story of Artemis and Orion and accepted the demand of the goddess, and we can see the giant hunter today as the constellation of Orion, close by, of course, the constellation Scorpius.

Callisto, Arcas and the Bears Constellations

Callisto, daughter of the King of Arcadia Lycaon was a nymph. As a follower of goddess Artemis, and one of her hunting attendants, she had taken a vow of celibacy. One day though Zeus saw her and fell in love with her. He turned into Artemis and used the goddess' authority on Callisto to take advantage of her. Then Callisto bore a son, Arcas. As usual, Hera decided to punish an innocent woman for the behavior of his husband, and so she turned Callisto into a bear.

Some years later, Callisto met her son Arcas, and in emotion ran towards him. The boy thought that she was just a normal bear and slayed her. Zeus, moved by their terrible fate, decided to turn Arcas too into a bear, and then to turn both the mother and the son into constellations, the Great Bear, also known as Ursa Major, and the Little Bear, also known as Ursa Minor.

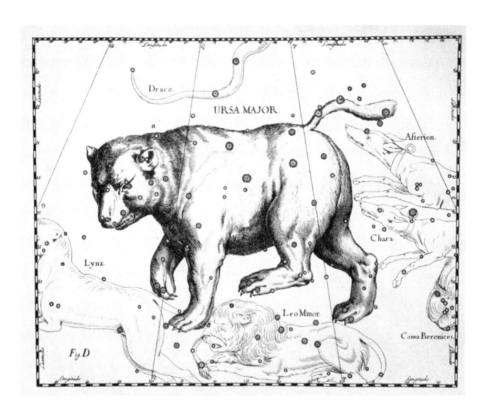

Johannes Hevelius - *Ursa Maior* - 1690

Heracles And The Origin Of The Milky Way

For a change, Zeus has had a son from a mortal woman, Alcmene. An indignant Hera then ordered Ilithyia, the Greek goddess of childbirth, to prevent Alcmene from giving birth. So Ilithyia told Alcmene to sit cross-legged and then tied her clothes with strong knots in order to prevent the woman from delivering. Alcmene's faithful servant Galanthis, though, told Ilithyia that Alcmene had already delivered the baby. Incredulous, the goddess untied the knots to check it herself, thus allowing Alcmene to give birth to a couple of twins, Heracles and Iphicles.

Alcmene and her husband Amphitryon, worried about the possible reaction of Hera, decided to hide Iphicles and expose Heracles in a Theban field. Athena decided to intervene in support of her half-brother so she came down from Mount Olympus, took up the newborn baby, and brought him home with her.

Once she saw the baby, Hera got past the anger, took the boy from Athena, and started to nurse him. Heracles suckled on Hera so hard that the goddess found it too painful and pushed the baby away. The milk spilled and sprayed across the universe, and the droplets formed the Milky Way. Heracles was gifted with divine powers since he was fed on the supernatural milk of Hera.

Peter Paul Rubens - *The Birth of the Milky Way* - 1637

Franz von Stuck - *Sisyphus* - 1920

Greek gods are quite far from the current idea we may have about deities. When we think of a deity we imagine them detached, superior, and indifferent to weaknesses, passions, pettinesses, and fears that afflict the human spirit. Truth is, Greek gods were as much superhuman regarding their powers as they were human regarding their passions. And it was not unusual for them to enter in competition with humans or direct on them their passions, jealousies, and outraged reactions, putting themselves on their same level. when not on a lower one.

Leto The Titan And The Tears Of Niobe

Niobe was the granddaughter of Zeus and daughter of Tantalus. She had a loving husband and fourteen children. In Greek mythology, though, many mortals met their downfall being punished for their pride and arrogance, for challenging the gods of Olympus or refusing to worship them.

Niobe, Queen of Thebes, was one such mortal. Her downfall began when she set herself above the Goddess Leto, the Titan.

Niobe was at a celebration to honor Leto, the mother of Artemis and Apollo. The temple was filled with worshippers who lit incense and prayed to Leto. For some reason, Niobe decided that competing with a Goddess in her own temple was the smartest thing to do. So she ordered her people to cease their silly behavior, claiming she was their queen, and to her, not to Leto, they should kneel, offering gifts, sacrifices, and vows of loyalty.

To top it off, Niobe also bragged about her own fourteen children, comparing that number to the only two of the goddess, and concluding that therefore she was more important. The wrath of Leto was great. So she sent her two children, the twins Apollo and Artemis, to teach Niobe a lesson. Apollo killed all seven of Niobe's sons with his powerful arrows in front of their mother's eyes.

Niobe began to scream with grief, but still, her pride took over, and she started waving her fist at the sky, yelling to the goddess Leto, for she still had seven daughters and Leto had only two.

Seven more arrows flew and felled the seven daughters of Niobe. This time the arrows came from Artemis' bow. Niobe was so overcome with grief that she couldn't move, she could just cry and cry.

Zeus felt sorry for her and transformed her into a rock, to turn her feelings into stone too, but even as a rock, Niobe continued to cry. To this day, Niobe is mourning for her children and someone says you may see a faint image of her carved on a limestone rock cliff on Mount Sipylus, with her ceaseless tears seeping in the form of water out of the porous rocks.

Philemon And Baucis

Baucis and her husband Philemon were a poor and old couple that lived in a rich and prosperous town in Phrygia, the same region King Midas used to rule upon. They had grown together living in a modest and shabby hut in the suburbs of the town. Their wealthy neighbors looked down on that poor couple, but they loved each other, and they were generous to other poor people.

One day, two men that looked worn out by a long journey arrived in that town after nightfall, looking for food and shelter. The two men, one old and the other one young knocked at the doors of all the rich and elegant houses, and every time they were driven off by watchdogs or guardians who had instructions not to let poor strangers disturb their noble masters, not during the day, let alone at night. At last, when they were almost up to lose faith, the two strangers knocked at the door of Baucis and Philemon's hut.

The door opened wide to receive them while a feeble voice welcomed the two strangers. With the poor means at his disposal, Philemon improvised a couch for the guests with thatch and reeds and spread the finest blanket, we may say the less worn out, over it. Then, he arranged a modest meal with what he could find from his garden and the few supplies from his modest kitchen.

While her husband was providing their guests with this first welcome, Baucis revived the fire to warm the two travelers and made them some soup and a couple of eggs. Then she pulled out from the shabby cupboard the two dishes in the better state and set out the things they'd saved as treats for the following feast day: some olives, dried fruit, a bit of honeycomb. Philemon also brought out the wine. It wasn't a fine wine and wine like that would have never found a place on the tables of their affluent neighbors, but it was the best they had.

The supper preparations were slow because the couple was old and tired, but they were nice to their guests and made some conversation as they worked to let the time run a little faster for the two travelers waiting. Then, when the meals were served, they tried everything possible to make sure their guests had enough food and were at ease.

But then they began to feel uncomfortable themselves, realizing that their cups of wine were refilling themselves, and with much better wine than they would have expected. The old couple looked anxious at each other and apologized to their visitors for offering such poor food. They felt so sorry for that, and if their guests would have been so patient to wait, they still had a goose who could be roasted.

The goose was a young and strong one, and she was not much into the idea of ending up roasted. The couple, on its side, was old and weak, so they chased the goose all around the hut but they weren't able to catch her. At last, she hid between the guests, who smiled, convinced their kind hosts to stop worrying and apologizing, and told them to just sit down, rest themselves, and let the goose live. The guests, they explained, did not need food anymore. They were gods. The older one revealed himself as Zeus, and the younger was his son Hermes. They had come to punish the town for its inhospitality and lack of generosity, but it was clear to them now that Philemon and Baucis deserved something better. They then asked the old couple to climb the slope behind the house with them.

Jean-Bernard Restout - *Philemon and Baucis Giving Hospitality to Jupiter and Mercury* - 1769

Philemon and Baucis went up the slope with difficulty and preceding rather behind their divine guests. When they reached the top of the slope and turned around to look down on the sleeping town, the town wasn't there anymore. A wide stretch of water took its place. They immediately looked at their hut, feeling sad at the idea of it swallowed by the water. But then they stared at it amazed. The hut was gone, but in its place stood a majestic temple with columns of marble and roofs of gold.

They turned back to look at their guests. Zeus smiled at them and told them to ask for whatever their hearts desired most as compensation for their selfless kindness. The old couple asked for a little time to talk about it, and the gods told them to take all the time they needed. Finally, they came back with their answer. What they wanted was to serve together in the temple that just appeared in place of their old hut, and that when their time came, they might die at the same moment so that neither of them would have to mourn the other.

Their wishes were granted. The story of the temple and the lake spread far and wide, and Philemon and Baucis welcomed pilgrims with the same generosity and hospitality they once reserved to the gods, but this time with better means of provision.

One day when they were very very old, Philemon and Baucis sat together in the sun in the temple courtyard, remembering that magical night in which their modest cottage disappeared to make way to the temple thanks to their marvelous guests. While they were all assorted in their memories, Baucis looked up and stared at her husband. Green branches were thrusting out from his shoulders. At that moment Philemon looked at her and he stared in wonder too, looking at her bright leaves. They had time to smile at each other one more time and to say a serene goodbye.

The pilgrims coming out from the temple saw no sign of the human guardians who had welcomed them. At their place, an oak tree and a linden tree stood close together as though they were embracing. The pilgrims then adorned their boughs with garlands and worshipped and praised the faithful couple who had praised and worshipped the gods since the temple was born.

The Midas Touch

Midas was the King of Phrygia, a prosperous kingdom in his day, rich in nature and well known for its flowers. One day the king's servants went out into his gardens and found a fat old drunk stinking of wine snoring amid the roses. Of course, he wasn't allowed to be in the royal gardens, but since he was rather obviously not a threat, the servants tied him up with flower-garlands instead of ropes, and hauled him in in front of the king, snickering all the while.

King Midas recognized the man: he was not an ordinary drunken mortal, but Silenus, the preceptor of Bacchus, the god of wine, and father of the satyrs. Midas had his servants immediately untie Silenus. By the time the old man was sober enough to know what was going on around him, he was not treated as a prisoner but as an honored guest. After ten days of feasting in honor of Silenus, Midas sent him back to Bacchus, who had begun to miss the old tutor. Bacchus, well pleased, told Midas to name any gift he wished for. Midas, not much wisely indeed, asked eagerly that whatever he touched with his hands should turn to gold.

Bacchus, sensing that the request of the king may lead to something unpleasant for Midas, asked him if he was sure about his wish. Midas was definitely sure: transforming everything in gold, what could have gone wrong? Bacchus grinned inwardly and told Midas that since he was that sure his wish was granted already. Midas reached out to touch a branch of a holm-oak above him. As he touched it, the branch turned to gold, it was beautiful to see and also very valuable.

Midas went home very excited and arrived bringing golden twigs, stones, and fruits he had collected on his way. He placed his hands on the doorposts and gloated seeing them turning into gold. He was so exhilarated he couldn't stop transforming things into gold just by touching them. So he went on for a while with his new activity, until a little appetite showed. So he went to the dining hall and sat down to eat...

It was only then that he realized the reason for Bacchus' skepticism. Because, of course, all the food he tried to get to his mouth turned to gold at his touch, becoming as shiny and precious as inedible. And when he tried to drink, his touch not only turned to gold the cup, but also the wine inside of it.

Midas thought again on Bacchus' strange expression and all the stories he had heard about how the gods disliked mortal greed came back to his mind. He realized what a fool he had been, and then desperately began to beg Bacchus to forgive his greedy wish.

Bacchus, whose character was more playful than vindictive, has been more amused than outraged by Midas' choice, and his aim was not really to punish the king but just making a little fun of him. The wine-god sent Midas to wash in the River Pactolus, and as the water washed the curse away the king cupped some of it in his hands and drank it. After all, he still got something important from the gift of Bacchus: the awareness of what is really important in life.

Icarus and Daedalus

The story of Icarus is kind of a parable and a cautionary tale on the dangers of pride and disobedience. Icarus was the son of Daedalus, that we remember as the great craftsman who created the Labyrinth for Minos to hide the Minotaur. Well, the fact is that Minos found out that it was Dedalus himself who advised Princess Ariadne to give Theseus the thread that helped him come out from the infamous Labyrinth after killing the Minotaur.

Minos was infuriated when found out about the betrayal and imprisoned Daedalus and his son Icarus in his own labyrinth. Daedalus was brilliant and inventive, and he immediately started thinking about how he and Icarus would escape the Labyrinth. The labyrinth he created was too complicated even for himself, so he did not consider the idea of just finding their way out. Also, he knew that the shores of Crete were perfectly guarded, so they would not be able to escape by sea either.

The only way left was the air, and so Daedalus managed to create gigantic wings of woven wicker kept together with wax. He taught Icarus how to use those wings to fly, and told him to stay away from the sun or the heat would have melted the wax and destroyed the wings. Daedalus and Icarus managed to escape the Labyrinth and flew free in the sky.

Although his father's warnings, Icarus was too young and too enthusiastic about flying. He got excited by the thrill of flying and carried away by the feeling of freedom. So he started flying high towards the sun and diving low to the sea, and then up high again, going higher every time. His father tried in vain to make young Icarus understand that his behavior was dangerous, but Icarus was too excited to listen.

Soon Icarus went too close to the sun and saw his wings melting. The boy fell into the sea and drowned. The sea where he fell was named after him and is still known as the Icarian Sea nowadays.

Jacob Peter Gowy - *The Fall of Icarus* - 1636

Sisyphus

Sisyphus was the founder and first king of Ephyra, today Corinth. He was a promoter of commerce and helped his city become a commercial hub by investing in navigation. In spite of the wealth he produced for his people, he wasn't a well-liked ruler because of his deceitful, sly, and avaricious character. On many occasions, he violated the Xenia, the Greek idea of sacred hospitality and generosity shown to travelers and guests of which we saw the utmost example in the myth of Philemon and Baucis. He used to kill his guests so he could prove that he was a ruthless king and stay in power reigning by terror.

These violations brought the king to the attention of Zeus, who was directly in charge of defending the Xenia. The father of gods wanted to punish Sisyphus for good so he asked Thanatos, the personification of death, to take the king of Ephyra and chain him in the Underworld. When Thanatos was about to give Sisyphus his punishment, the king asked how the chains actually worked, and with a trick, while Thanatos was showing him the functioning of the chains, Sisyphus swiftly managed to chain Thanatos instead.

With Death itself in chains, no mortal on earth could die and go to the Underworld anymore. After a while, the situation worsened, and the god of war Ares, seeing that his wars have become pointless as no one could die, released Thanatos. He then trapped Sisyphus and gave him back to Thanatos.

After a while, the king tricked Persephone, queen of the underworld, into releasing him and sending him back to the living, just as long as he needed to punish his wife for something she did. Persephone agreed, Sisyphus went back to the realm of the living, found his wife, and scolded her, but when the time came he refused to go back to Tartarus.

Finally the gods' messenger Hermes took him and dragged him back, but Zeus, who couldn't bear Sisyphus' tricks and hubris anymore decided to punish him for good. Now the cunning king was forced to eternally push a boulder uphill, and as soon as he would reach the top of the hill, the boulder would roll off and Sisyphus had to push it back again and again until the end of times.

Tiziano - *Sisyphus* - 1548

Deucalion and the Great Flood

Though he was chained to a mountain getting his liver eaten out all day, Prometheus did not lose sight of his beloved humans. He noticed that they had slowly become more and more evil and greedy. They were constantly at war and weren't respecting the gods as they should. Prometheus knew that Zeus was not happy with such a situation, so he warned his son, Deucalion, that the king of gods was angry and intended to destroy the earth. The punishment would take the form of a flood. So Prometheus told Deucalion to build a ship and fill it with supplies and an ember of fire.

Deucalion obeyed, and with his wife, Pyrrha, he went home to build a boat. The craft had just been finished when Zeus began to inundate the earth with a huge flood. It rained continuously for nine days and nine nights until the tops of the mountains remained the sole lands above water level. All of humanity drowned, except for Deucalion and his wife.

As the waters receded, the couple of survivors headed their boat toward Mount Parnassus. When they finally reached the mainland, they used the ember to light a fire and offer gratitude to the gods. After that tribute to the gods, Deucalion asked for permission to repopulate the planet.

Zeus was moved from the request of these two last humans on earth and told them to pick up the rocks near them on the ground. Then he commanded them to start walking and, at each step, to throw a stone behind them. Deucalion and Pyrrha carried out the task as instructed. On the spot of each rock thrown by Deucalion, a man came to life. Women, in the same way, were born from each stone thrown by Pyrrha. These new humans were stronger, wiser, and more respectful of the gods than the ones who had perished in the flood.

Apollo and Daphne

It is commonly said that Daphne was the first love of Apollo but the truth is that the girl never reciprocated the god's love. Most nymphs and mortals were attracted to the handsome Apollo, but the one they loved rejected them. But let's see how it all started.

Francesco Albani - *Apollo and Daphne* - 1615

One day Apollo was teasing Eros about his bow and arrow telling that he did not believe it may actually work, so the love god shot a golden arrow into the god's heart. The arrow caused Apollo to fall in love with Daphne, a beautiful river nymph and devotee of Artemis, Apollo's twin sister. Apollo chased the nymph through the forest, pleading for her to stop and spend some time with him, but she kept running. She was a virgin, a follower of Artemis, and she devoted her life to the woods.

But finally, Apollo caught her. Resolute to preserve her virginity, Daphne called her father to protect her. And her father, a river god, could not figure out any smarter solution than transforming his daughter into a laurel tree, and so he did. Daphne's feet rooted to the ground, her arms became branches, leaves started growing from her fingers, and bark grew across her torso.

Apollo was heart-broken at the loss of Daphne, and to remember her forever he made the laurel the symbol of tribute to poets. The laurel became, therefore, the symbol of the god himself being Apollo the god of (among many other things) poetry.

Eros and Psyche

Psyche was the youngest and most gorgeous of three princesses. Her beauty was famous and men from all Greece set off on a journey just to see her, many of them said that Psyche was even lovelier than the goddess of beauty Aphrodite herself.

Unsurprisingly this comparison upset Aphrodite. So she asked her son, Eros, to make the girl fall in love with someone really ugly. Eros went to Psyche to carry out his mother's request, but once he approached her, he was struck by her beauty and fell in love with her.

One day Psyche's father consulted the oracle of Delphi to ask who his most beautiful daughter would marry. Eros talked Apollo into making the oracle tell the father that Psyche would become the wife of a terrible winged serpent. This was her fate, and to do that, Psyche, dressed in black, should be brought to the summit of a mountain and stay there alone until her monstrous future husband would come up and take her for his wife.

Psyche accepted her fate and climbed to the top of the mountain, lonely and afraid, to wait for the beast. The dragon did not show up and the beautiful princess fell asleep. When she woke up, she found herself near a beautiful mansion. She heard some voices telling her to go inside, that she did. Once in she took a bath and had some delicious food.

Then she went to bed, and her monstrous new husband joined her. Psyche was terrified but she found out with surprise that the monster was actually a sweet and tender lover. She couldn't see him, but he was kind to her and his voice was pleasant. He seemed to be everything Psyche had always dreamed of her husband, absolutely far from a horrible serpent, and the princess grew to love him. Each night she ended up in his arms, and she was happy about that though she never saw his face.

Psyche's sisters grew jealous of her happiness. They told her she should not trust her mysterious husband. She never could see him and according to the prophecy, he could have been a winged serpent in disguise. In the end they convinced Psyche to find out what was behind that mystery. So that night, when she went to bed, she brought a lamp and a knife with her, intended to find out who her husband was. And if he were a monster, she was prepared to kill him.

That night he came to her like every other night, speaking words of love, but this time, when he fell asleep, she used the lamp to look upon his face. Far from being an awful winged serpent, he was the most handsome man she had ever seen. She gasped in surprise and accidentally spilled a drop of hot oil from the lamp on his shoulder. He awoke and ran away without saying a word.

Then Psyche heard a voice telling her the truth about her husband: he was Eros, the god of love, and son of Aphrodite. She then began looking for him, and she searched all over the world. Distraught, she sought Eros' mother's help, unaware of the role played by the jealous goddess all along. Aphrodite told her that she was willing to help, but in order to do that, she asked Psyche to complete four tasks. She was hoping that the hard work would make Psyche's beauty fade and her son's love for her with it.

As the first trial, Psyche had to sort a pile of mixed grain into three separate heaps of barley, oats, and wheat by sunset. She despaired because the task seemed impossible to bring to an end, but the ants helped her and she delivered her task on time.

The second trial was to cross a river and shear the golden wool from a flock of vicious sheep. Again, she despaired at first, but the reeds along the bank of the river took the sheep's wool when they came to drink, and let her gather it.

The third task was to collect water in a crystal bottle from the river Styx's source. The rocks were slippery and dangerous, but this time came to help an eagle sent by Zeus that took her bottle from her hands, filled it at the source, and returned it to her full.

Finally, for the fourth task, Aphrodite sent Psyche to the underworld, telling her to bring back a box with a sample of Persephone's beauty in it. The goddess had to use much of her beauty to heal the burn her son got from the oil spilled from the lamp, and now she needed some of Persephone's. Psyche once again despaired, this seemed really impossible, but she did not give up, exhausted she arrived in the realm of the dead, where the queen of the underworld, seemingly moved by her story, agreed to place some of her beauty in the box.

As Psyche returned to Aphrodite's temple, just like the goddess plan foreseen, her beauty had begun to fade. Now that she was about to have her love back, she was losing most of her beauty. She was desperate, and in a moment of weakness, she opened the box, planning to use just a little part of Persephone's beauty and hoping that Aphrodite wouldn't notice. But it turned out that the box contained not Persephone's beauty, but the sleep of the dead, and Psyche fell to the ground.

Luckily, by this time, Eros had healed and having understood her plan escaped from his mother. He found a dead-looking Psyche but woke her from the enchanted sleep with a kiss. Psyche delivered the box to Aphrodite, who at last relented. Eros asked Zeus to make Psyche immortal. Psyche and Eros got married and lived happily ever after.

Orpheus and Eurydice

The young mortal Orpheus was the most talented musician on the planet. Amazing singer and skillful lyre player, he was the son of Apollo, after whom he took his extreme talent in music, and the Muse Calliope. No god or mortal could resist his music, and even the rocks and trees would move themselves to be near him whenever he performed. Animals would gather in ecstatic attention, and even the rivers would change course to listen to its poignant, beautiful melodies. Jason recruited him to sail with the Argonauts, and energize the heroes during their quest with his enchanting music.

At some point Orpheus fell in love with a young woman named Eurydice, hence, inspired by this deep love, his music became even more beautiful. But one day, on what was supposed to be the happiest day of their lives, their wedding day, as the couple walked through a meadow, a poisonous snake bit Eurydice's heel, who died almost immediately.

Gaetano Gandolfi - *Orpheus and Eurydice* - 1802

In grief, Orpheus vowed to get her back from the realm of the dead. Very very few ever entered the underworld and returned, but Eurydice's death was so tragic and unjust that Orpheus was convinced that the gods must have made a mistake.

The musician set off on a journey to recover his bride. With his lyre, he charmed Charon, the boatman of the river Styx who separated the realm of the dead from the realm of the living, and he carried him across. With his mesmerizing melodies, he subdued Cerberus, the three-headed dog that guards the gates of the Underworld. Finally, he reached Hades and Persephone, and he made his honest and courageous request to the god of the Underworld. He knew Eurydice now belonged to Hades but he wanted to have her back until her days on earth would naturally come to an end. To try to persuade Hades, Orpheus sang about how much he loved Eurydice, reminding Hades of his love for Persephone.

Hades was moved by the voice of Orpheus and by the memories of his own love, and he granted the musician's wish. He called Eurydice and told Orpheus he could lead her back to the world of the living, but with one caveat: She would follow him and he couldn't look at her until they reached the land of the living. If he did, he'd lose her forever.

Orpheus began to lead Eurydice on the long journey back toward the sunlight while playing his lyre and fighting the urge to look back. As the couple finally neared the land of the living, Orpheus stepped out of the darkness and spun around to see his love again.

But he had turned too early. Eurydice had not yet stepped out of the shadows of the underworld. He gasped in horror realizing what a tragic mistake he just made, but it was too late, she faded away, gone forever.

Atalanta The Hunter

Atalanta's father had always wanted a son, so when a little girl was born, he ordered his servants to abandon her on a mountain. Atalanta was raised by a mother bear and became a fast, strong girl. When the hunters saw her skills, they recognized her potential and showed her how to shoot an arrow and throw a spear.

She became the most beautiful woman in Arcadia and one of its strongest, fastest, and most powerful hunters. Atalanta became a follower of Artemis and took the oath of virginity, which meant she had always to fight off potential suitors.

In nearby Calydon, King Oeneus forgot to make the sacrifice to Athena, so the goddess sent a giant boar to terrorize his kingdom. The boar killed or wounded all the best hunters in Calydon, so the king decided to recruit all the greatest hunters from abroad to kill it, promising the boar's hide to whoever slays the beast. Among the dozens of men who arrived from all over to participate in the contest and win the prestigious prize, there was one woman: Atalanta. Most of the men found it unacceptable to have to hunt with a woman, but Meleager, the king's son, fell in love with her.

The hunt began, and soon the boar attacked. Atalanta was the only one brave enough to stand her ground and fire an arrow at it, while all the men ran away. She wounded the beast, enabling Meleager to slay it with his spear. Meleager credited Atalanta with the kill and gave her the boar's hide, which enraged everyone because no one would admit a woman's superiority. The disagreement resulted in a fight, and Meleager ended up fighting and killing his uncles.

Many years before, the Fates had predicted to Meleager's mother that his son would only live as long as a certain log in her fireplace would not have burned. Like any protective mother, she took the log off the fire and hid it. But once he killed her brothers, she didn't want to protect her own son anymore. She took the log out and tossed it into the flames, and Meleager died.

As for Atalanta, the word of her boar-killing success attracted even more attention from men. She was still committed to virginity and had no interest in companionship, so she announced she would only marry the man who could beat her in a race. Many men tried, and she even gave them a head start to make it interesting, but they always lost—and many of them also died from the exertion.

Finally, a man named Hippomenes asked Aphrodite's help for the race. The goddess of love thought Atalanta's obsession with virginity was foolish, so she gave Hippomenes three golden apples. As Atalanta and Hippomenes raced, the man dropped the first two apples. Two times she slowed down to pick them up but would always catch up to him again. In desperation, Hippomenes threw the last apple as far as he could from the finish line, and as Atalanta got into the woods to chase the fruit, he rushed ahead and won by a hair. Impressed by his cleverness and speed, Atalanta agreed to marry him, and they lived happily ever after... or at least until Cybele turned them into lions for copulating too close to her temple.

Willem van Herp - *Atalanta and Hippomenes* - 1650

CONCLUSION

So here we are. Our journey into Greek mythology is over. Or, at least, the piece of the walk we took together.

My wish is that this may have been for you the first step on a long path. This book is nothing more than what I promised it would be: a collection of stories. Plain and simple, in an easy language, and with no explanations or interpretations.

Just stories for the sake of the stories, because Greek mythology deserves to be given that: apart from its religious, pedagogical, psychological, social, or historical meanings they are just great stories that formed us and that deserve to be narrated, and read, as such.

That being said, if this book should spark in you the flame of a new passion, well, I couldn't be happier. I like to think that some of my readers decided to further read about the many aspects of Greek myth, and maybe one day think back to that simple little book that started everything. And I like to think that this reader might be you.

Still, if you just enjoyed a few pleasant hours in the company of pleasant stories, well, I would know my job is done.

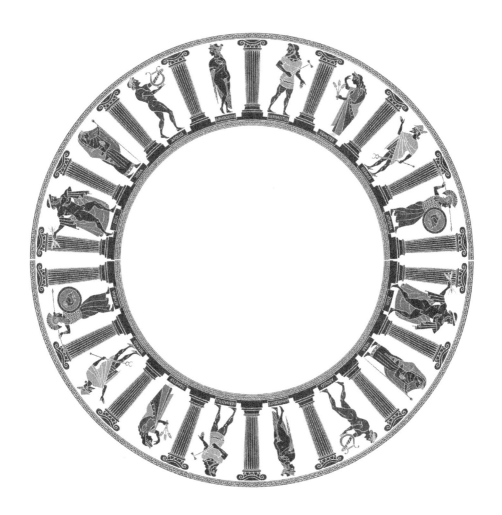

Printed in Great Britain
by Amazon

13801709R00119